Southern Workhorses
No.1 Q 0-6-0s 30530-30549

Leslie Tibble
Richard Derry

30544 at Three Bridges shed in September 1952. H.C. Casserley, courtesy M. Casserley.

Irwell Press Ltd.

ACKNOWLEDGEMENTS

Special thanks to Mike King and to Eric Youldon; also Nick Deacon, Peter Groom, Allan Baker, Derek Phillips, Gavin Glenister, Ian Sixsmith, Neil Knowlden. Richard Derry constructed the tables with customary assiduity. The Southern Railways Group was formed over 40 years ago to study and disseminate information about the Southern Railway, British Railways (Southern Region), its successors and minor railways in southern England. Publications include data sheets, a bi-monthly newsletter, and a quarterly magazine. Membership applications via the website (http://srg.org.uk/) or to the Hon. Membership Secretary: membersec@srg.org.uk

First published in the United Kingdom in 2019,
by Irwell Press Limited, 59A, High Street, Clophill,
Bedfordshire MK45 4BE
Tel: 01525 861888
www.irwellpress.com

Southern Workhorses
No.1 Q 0-6-0s 30530-30549

BEGINNINGS

This entirely traditional and unremarkable British 0-6-0, metaphorically and actually, was Maunsell's 'last fling' and construction had not even begun when Bulleid succeeded him as Chief Mechanical Engineer of the Southern Railway. The order for the engines had been placed in March 1936 but the first, 530, did not appear for nearly two years, until January 1938 way after Maunsell had retired through ill health in 1937. Bulleid would have cancelled production if he'd taken up office on the SR earlier (it is recorded) but you'd have to think there was enough time to bring the work to a halt or to redesign the locos if he really wanted to, and he didn't. So the coming of these twenty very ordinary 0-6-0s over January 1938-September 1939 was hardly an earthquake in the world of locomotive design; barely a tremor in fact and indeed they had a distinctly pre-Grouping look about them. Their entirely traditional outline made the succeeding Bulleid Q1 seem even more bizarre; did he consciously (or unconsciously) strive to make *his* 0-6-0 as *unlike* the preceding design as possible?

Like other railways the Southern had used older, obsolete types for secondary and branch line work but everything must come to an end in time and a number, particularly Adams 0-4-2s going back to the 1880s, the 'Jubilees', were still staggering gamely about the system and would at last have to be replaced. There were ageing 0-6-0s too, very much in need of replacement. The provision of twenty thoroughly traditional 0-6-0s was thus in a way a perfectly explicable solution; after all such locos (or the tank equivalent on the GWR) were the mainstay of branch line, pick up work and much else that was similar across the country.

The new locos were barely above the notice of *The Railway Magazine* and in March 1937 it merely remarked: *The twenty 0-6-0 tender goods engines in the 1937 locomotive programme will be classified as class Q nos.530-549 and will be built at Eastleigh. They are to have side window cabs.* The grand old organ was more forthcoming a year later, in March 1938, carrying a photograph of the initial example, 530 under the heading *New 0-6-0 Goods Engines for the Southern Railway.* They were, it was noted *...considerably more powerful than the old engines they will replace*

which was pretty much usual for a new class. They were in fact the first 0-6-0 design for the Southern Railway. Tractive effort, a not particularly useful measure of itself, was given as 26,157lb, ten per cent or so beyond the contemporaneous LMS 4F: *A Sinoflo superheater is fitted … the 19in by 26in inside cylinders have long travel piston valves of 10in diameter operated by Stephenson valve motion through rocking levers; steam reversing gear is fitted.* The superheater was a 'Maunsell superheater', the trade name Sinoflo referring to the manufacturer of the superheater tubes. Despite the 'goods' description, in fact they were often used on passenger duties; indeed they *intended* to be proper mixed traffic locos and indeed were so for much of their lives. While *The Railway Magazine* might have described them as goods engines, the *Southern Railway Magazine* was better informed: *The engines being of general utility, are equipped with steam heating connections at each end for passenger train working when required.*

The look of a Q recalled much of the L1 4-4-0 and the N 2-6-0, the close family resemblance deriving from the sharing of obviously Maunsell

The new 0-6-0 posed for the record. Until change came under Bulleid the engines carried the rather curious combination of oval number plate on the cab, SOUTHERN in a serif, and number on the tender in a block style. In addition there was a sort of serif number on the tender rear and a serif number on the front buffer beam. It would have been hard to misidentify one of them. The angular outline of the framing at the front is always remarked-upon; subsequent engines had a curving style.

There were at least two new Q 0-6-0s at Eastleigh shed on 15 October 1938 and 533 (to traffic July) and 534 (August-September) reveal the serif numbers on the tender rear and the front buffer beam. So a Q, like other SR locos, had no less than *six* numbers! Note how the running plate and valence is 'waisted' in about mid-way. Both had gone new to Eastleigh. H.C. Casserley, courtesy M. Casserley.

New 535 at where else but Eastleigh on the same day, 15 October 1938; certainly a contrast in tenders and chimneys and the positioning of lettering on engines either side... H.C. Casserley, courtesy M. Casserley.

features like the cab, smokebox, firebox and chimney. It had standard parts in common with the N 2-6-0 and the L1 4-4-0 but was not a standard class. S.C. Cocks, in his paper to the Institution of Locomotive Engineers of 1948, *History of Southern Railway Locomotives to 1938* writes of the Q: *In 1934 consideration was given to the renewal of boilers for the C class and 700 class and similar engines. Owing to the age of these engines, it was thought better to look into the modification of class 700 to enable the C class to be replaced. In 1936 authority was received to proceed with the building of twenty goods locomotives to replace the 700 and C classes, called the Q class. The design generally is based on the L1 and N class for detail parts. These engines are of the type generally used throughout the country, without any outstanding features except that the valves are outside admission (which was used to give easy exhaust) as compared with the more general inside admission, and are actuated by Stephenson valve gear.*

SOME Q DETAIL
Frames
As is so often the case detail differences were apparent right from

the appearance of the second engine. The first, 530, had an angular outline to the framing at the front, while the rest emerged with a somewhat more graceful curve. Late on, as 30530, the original loco acquired the 'curved' frames – presumably a spare set held at Eastleigh. If these angular original frames were re-used, so far they have not been spotted on any other Q.

Tenders
The tenders with which the engines entered service were not new and though the original order included twenty 4,000 gallon tenders the intention was to run these with N class 1407-1414 and U class 1618-1629. Second-hand 3,500 gallon, straight sided, six wheeled tenders (5 tons of coal) were instead transferred to the 0-6-0s from U class 2-6-0s 1610-1629, suitably altered to match the left-hand drive 0-6-0s. The price of £7,200 for each Q included a sum for each of these twenty new 4,000 gallon tenders with which they were not intended to run. In some instances the second-hand tenders could not be made immediately available and the completed Q was parked at

Eastleigh for a week or so before its tender arrived from Ashford.

Q tenders from U 2-6-0s		
Q	**No.**	**U**
530	1904	1614
531	1901	1611
532	1900	1610
533	1907	1617
534	1903	1613
535	1905	1615
536	1919	1629
537	1911	1621
538	1902	1612
539	1906	1616
540	1908	1618
541	1909	1619
542	1910	1620
543	1915	1625
544	1912	1622
545	1914	1624
546	1916	1626
547	1913	1628
548	1917	1627
549	1894	1804

Tender Cab
536 acquired an experimental 'tender cab' for protection during tender-first

530, near to Southampton Terminus, in July 1938. The angular front frame extensions are clear. They were there to provide room for lifting holes but as these were rarely if ever used all further Qs were built minus the extensions. Late in life 530, by then 30530, was bought into line; perhaps they got in the way of a snowplough attachment. Frank Foote, courtesy Mike King.

533 at Eastleigh, September 1938. Frank Foote, courtesy Mike King.

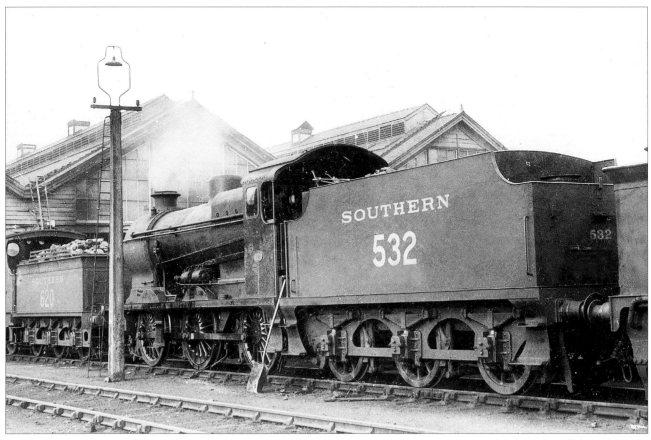

Another new Q at Eastleigh, on 15 October 1938; number on tender rear. 532 stayed at Eastleigh until well into the War, though in a sense the place was the 'first shed' of every Q in that all were run in from there. It was back working from Eastleigh at the War's end and ended up one of only two examples to work from Salisbury, for its last few months in 1962-63. Rail washer pipe visible for once (with the eye of faith) behind the trailing coupled wheel. H.C. Casserley, courtesy M. Casserley.

The Bulleid livery as applied to 541, at Norwood Junction on 28 July 1945; black, with the 'sunshine' lettering. These are the last months for the original chimneys and in the case of 541 the multiple jet blastpipe will appear at the end of the following year. Of interest is the blanked-off cab side window, an anti-glare device for the duration of the blackout during the war years. H.C. Casserley, courtesy M. Casserley.

Bulleid livery on 542 at Tunbridge Wells West on 9 August 1947 – blackout plate still in place more than two years after the lifting of the blackout. H.C. Casserley, courtesy M. Casserley.

running in June 1947. This seems to have taken the form of sheets at the rear of the cab, both sides, with windows. This would have restricted working room in the cab which is probably why the arrangement was dispensed with a few months later, in September. If protection was to be provided for tender-first running, the answer was to build it into the front of the tender, as in the case of some LMS 4Fs for instance.

Boilers
Twenty boilers, numbered 1064-1083 were completed at Eastleigh Works for the Qs, a smaller version of that fitted to the L1, very slightly tapered with a Belpaire firebox. Two more, numbered 1084 and 1085 were completed in June, 1940 and September, 1940 respectively; 1084 was fitted to 548 (30/3/42-10/6/42) and 1085 to 537 (18/8/42-19/9/42) both at Eastleigh Works.

Chimneys
Bulleid had acquiesced in the building of the class but thought to improve performance in service and in due course, during its 19/8/40-6/11/40 visit to Eastleigh, 531 was fitted with a Lemaitre multiple jet blastpipe and a large diameter chimney – squat and ugly to some, bold and

Q DIMENSIONS	
Cylinders	19in stroke x 26in diameter
Boiler barrel	10ft 9^9/$_{16}$in
Barrel diameter	4ft 7¾in to 5ft
Maximum width of engine	8ft 4in
Width over cab sides	7ft 9 ^{3}/$_8$in
Height to chimney	12ft 10in
Driving wheels	5ft 1in diameter
Wheelbase	8ft + 8ft 6in = 16ft 6in
Heating surfaces	
Small tubes	158 x 1¾in
Super tubes	21 x 5 ^{1}/$_8$in
Total	1,125 sq ft
Firebox	122 sq ft
Total	1,247 sq ft [evaporative] Plus superheater of 185 sq ft = 1,432 sq ft
Grate area	21.9 sq ft
Working pressure	200 lbs psi
Tractive effort	26,160 lb
Engine weight in working order	
Leading drivers	18 tons
Middle drivers	18 tons
Rear drivers	13 tons 10 cwt
Total	49 tons 10 cwt
Tender weight in working order	
Leading wheels	13 tons 15 cwt
Middle wheels	13 tons 5 cwt
Rear wheels	13 tons10 cwt
Total	40 tons 10 cwt
Engine and tender	90 tons

BRITISH RAILWAYS in the sunshine style, as demonstrated on 30535 at Eastleigh, 9 July 1949. H.C. Casserley, courtesy M. Casserley.

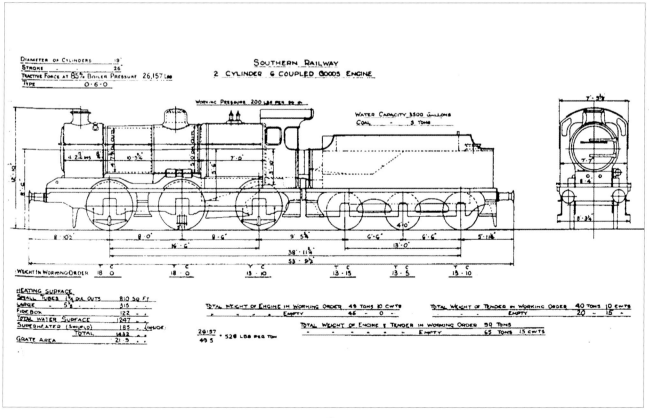

SOUTHERN RAILWAY
2 CYLINDER 6 COUPLED GOODS ENGINE

DIAMETER OF CYLINDERS	19"
STROKE	26"
TRACTIVE FORCE AT 85% BOILER PRESSURE	26,157 LBS
TYPE	0-6-0

WORKING PRESSURE 200 LBS PER SQ IN

WATER CAPACITY 3500 GALLONS
COAL — 5 TONS

HEATING SURFACE

SMALL TUBES 1¾ DIA OUTS	810 SQ FT
LARGE 5½"	315 "
FIRE BOX	122 "
TOTAL WATER SURFACE	1247 "
SUPERHEATER (SINGLE)	185 " (INSIDE)
TOTAL	1432 "
GRATE AREA	21.9 "

26157 ÷ 49.5 = 528 LBS PER TON

WEIGHT IN WORKING ORDER	18.0	18.0	13.10	13.15	13.5	13.10

TOTAL WEIGHT OF ENGINE IN WORKING ORDER 49 TONS 10 CWTS
EMPTY 45 — 0 —

TOTAL WEIGHT OF TENDER IN WORKING ORDER 40 TONS 10 CWTS
EMPTY 20 — 15 —

TOTAL WEIGHT OF ENGINE & TENDER IN WORKING ORDER 90 TONS
EMPTY 65 TONS 15 CWTS

At first there were no BR tender lettering transfers (for the design hadn't been decided upon) and there were no cast smokebox plates either, so the number was painted on the buffer beam in a sort of mix of 'sunshine' and block, as on light engine 30534 waiting here to leave London Bridge on 30 September 1948. It would have worked in on a passenger train from Tunbridge Wells and has helped push the stock out of the platform – at a guess that is the tail end of its train (a birdcage set) disappearing at right. The Qs were used on Tunbridge Wells West-London Bridge/Victoria trains from about 1945 until the arrival of the Fairburn 2-6-4Ts in 1950. 30534, 30542, 30543, 30544 were the regulars. LeMaître chimney installed a few months before, 'B' power classification visible behind the buffer beam this end. B.W.L. Brooksbank, Initial Photographics.

dashingly French to others. The locomotive was then used on local goods and demonstrated improvements in steaming. When working hard there was said to be 'much fire throwing' which would have put up coal consumption. Adjustments must have been successfully applied for after the war this became a standard fitment and the performance of the locos accordingly improved.

During a General Overhaul 29/6/55-6/8/55 at Eastleigh 30549 was fitted with a BR class 4 plain blastpipe and stovepipe in place of the Lemaitre. This looked plain ugly and rather than a stovepipe chimney proper, was in fact the inner sleeve of a conventional BR chimney.

30549's new arrangements improved performance and several others were also dealt with, 30530 30536, 30538, 30543, 30545 and 30547; happily in their case a BR standard form of chimney was used, to the engines' vastly better appearance. The majority

Continues page 16.

Transition to 'BR Sunshine' on 542 now, on 30542 at Stewarts Lane in 1948 not long after a General (A) completed in May that year. H.C. Casserley, courtesy M. Casserley.

30543, a birdcage 3-set in tow and again newly fitted with LeMaître exhaust, has a similarly adorned buffer beam to that of 30534, in a fine portrait very much making the point that the engines were mixed traffic, if only on weekends! The train is a down London Bridge-Tunbridge Wells West via Hever working, coming under Purley Downs Road bridge just north of Riddlesdown station, in the winter of 1948-49. These must have been the only 0-6-0 tender engines working main line passenger trains out of major London stations; certainly in the BR era and for many decades before that. Two bolted plates at the front under the smokebox door could be removed to afford access to the cylinder heads and piston rods. Each had two handles, as visible here, to manhandle the plates off once unbolted.

Weathered 30540 at Three Bridges, 10 June 1950. Under that dirt are remnants of the sunshine lettering; the new number was applied (March 1949) but the tender kept its SOUTHERN. A bright spark has thought to polish up the S and R of SOUTHERN to denote Southern Region! H.C. Casserley, courtesy M. Casserley.

Concerning BR emblems/crests (Eric Youldon writes) two sizes of the first lion to wheel version were authorised, in an Instruction dated 23 June 1949; large (16 inch diameter wheel) for Pacifics, Lord Nelsons, King Arthurs, Schools, WD 2-8-0s, S15s and other 4-6-0s and moguls and also the two SR 0-6-0 classes, Q and Q1. A small (9 inch diameter) wheel was specified for all other classes. In a few weeks K 2-6-0s and Atlantics were added to the 'large' category. This didn't last long and an Instruction of 31 March 1950 specified that only the Pacifics, Nelsons, WDs and Q1s should get the larger emblem, everything else to be the smaller version. In the fullness of time Pacific tenders got the smaller emblems when the tender was cut down. Two subsequent transgressions are well known, G16 4-8-0T getting the large emblem in 1949 and Lord Nelson 30857 the small version in 1952. When the second emblem duly came along in March 1957 discipline was lax and whether large or small version appeared on say, the Qs, was much less strictly proscribed – see examples hereabouts.

Large first emblem on 30544, at Eastleigh on 21 October 1950. H.C. Casserley, courtesy M. Casserley.

30542 at Bournemouth shed on 17 July 1958, with the now-specified small lion and wheel emblem. The *Southern Railway Magazine* described the tender as 'of the standard N class' which was more or less factual. A.E. West, courtesy Mike King.

30544 new out of a General at the nearby works, at Eastleigh MPD on 18 September 1960. New coat of black, with the small second emblem. Richard Vitler Collection.

Another Q sparkling in newly-applied black, inevitably at Eastleigh MPD; 30541 on 25 August 1957 after a General which has seen the large second emblem applied. Various joins and rivets are visible along the top of the Q tenders, at what are sometimes called the 'raves'. Corrosion/welded repairs made parts visible, as here, that were largely invisible on other examples – especially when obscured by accumulated layers of grime. The end of the reversing shaft is visible just by the framing behind the middle splasher, close where the water feed pipe passes along and up to the clack valves on the boiler side. R.C. Riley, transporttreasury

A similar view, this time of 30548, transformed in appearance by years of dirt, at Eastleigh on 26 August 1963. An entire, new, plate has been fitted to the tender 'rave' this time; the reversing shaft is clearly visible. The oil delivery pipes ran down from the cab, contained along the side of the firebox in a distinctively shaped length of channelling. Needless to say this saw some variations over the years, as is apparent, actually, just in a comparison of these two, 30541 and 30548. Peter Groom.

The driver's side – the two openings low down indicate the presence of AWS equipment. The white (actually yellow) spot below the number is an indication that the loco has been equipped for water treatment, in the form of briquettes dropped in the tender tank, initiated by the Southern in the mid-1950s. A comparison with the left-hand cabside of 30548 with others reveals that the numbers were not always precisely in the same position relative to the various nuts. So on a model there is latitude in the positioning of the number transfers! Ron Cover.

That Snowplough Business 1. From late 1962, just as the first Qs were being withdrawn, a number were fitted up with substantial snowploughs. This was something of a departure from traditional practice; at various places around the country a shed might fit a few engines with small buffer-mounted ploughs or one or two with more substantial ploughs, to be taken off and stored once the threat of snow had gone. Fitting was done locally, so that some ploughs were unofficially given the numbers of 'their' loco, the only one it would fit. These Qs, it was envisaged, would keep the ploughs and until snow was forecast, would effectively be in store – which is why most photographs show them out of use in some out of the way siding. Not so 30536 (with standard BR Class 4 chimney) at Norwood Junction on 26 January 1963; as remarked on earlier, by great luck or unique meteorological insight, the 'Q Ploughs' were ready for the worst winter since 1947. A. Scarsbrook, Initial Photographics.

That Snowplough Business 2. 30545 stabled at Redhill on 9 February 1964. 'Snowplough details' were 'marked off' according to the Engine record in time for New year 1964 but as the weather was fairly mild, 30545 probably saw no use as a plough that winter – maybe never again, for it was withdrawn in April 1965, last but one of its tribe, though not before it could take part in the LCGB Maunsell Commemorative Tour in January that year. RailOnline

were done at the end of 1961, obviously a little late for any meaningful return.

Sanding
Steam sanders were fitted to the front of the leading driving wheels and behind the middle set of drivers while behind the rear set of driving wheels could be found that elusive animal, a de-sander or rail washer – it delivered a steam jet for rail cleaning after the application of sand – if deemed appropriate by the driver. Tender sanding is also recorded as having been fitted in the later days of BR; this was gravity-delivered sand to the front of the tender, again at the judgement of the driver. In poor adhesion conditions it prevented tender wheels from 'picking up' –

when braking caused wheels to lock up and therefore skid. This could happen when rails were wet and the tender was relatively light, when coal and water were low.

Livery and Numbering
Regarded as goods engines, the Q1s carried black livery with SOUTHERN in serif and number on the tender. With Bulleid came the 'sunshine' style and cabside numerals. After 1948 SOUTHERN gave way first to BRITISH RAILWAYS again in 'Sunshine' style. BR power classification was 4F and the livery officially BR black. 30000 was added to the running numbers to give 30530-30549 and numberplates were fitted to the smokebox.
535 and 544 emerged from overhaul

at Eastleigh before the BR renumbering carrying the short-lived s prefix; s535 from 7/2/48 (renumbered 30535 April 1950), s544 from 6/3/48 and (renumbered 30544 early 1950).

Reversing Gear
From new the engines were fitted with Stirling steam reversing gear, a singular piece of equipment not generally seen in British practice. It is the most obvious feature of a Q, astride the left-hand centre splasher, with the unmistakable pair of cylinders. It was complicated to use, apparently, or at least it would have seemed so to crews that did not see a Q that often and wear and maintenance shortcomings also caused problems. In its 'A' overhaul at Eastleigh October-December 1941 536 was fitted with '…a single lever

30538 in Eastleigh for a Light Casual, October 1961. Its Bulleid chimney stands forlornly in the foreground while somewhere out of sight is the waiting replacement BR Class 4 chimney and blastpipe. Only odd parts are being attended to, for example only the trailing wheelset has been removed, probably due to excessive axlebox wear in the horn guides. The right leading sandbox has been taken off and is lying alongside – some crack detection work seems to be underway on the framing behind it; hence the white colour. The oxy-acetylene equipment suggests some cutting has been done, probably the rivets locating the horn guides on the trailing axle. Notice the ladder has the chargehand's name – L SHEPHERD – painted on; such useful items were ripe for disappearing if not so identified in all erecting shops, with some unscrupulous individuals not averse to painting out and changing the names! The engine behind is one of Bulleid's Q1 class (a *Charlie One* as the men often referred to them as they were originally numbered C1 etc) also perhaps, undergoing a casual repair, although in this case all the wheelsets have been removed, along with the lagging sheets on the firebox. A typical erecting shop view from the steam age with all the other impedimenta laying around; one speculates what today's Health & Safety brigade have to say about that! The occasion is probably a Sunday enthusiast visit as there are no staff around.

30546 amid the Ivatts at Eastleigh on 2 July 1961.

controlling the reverser' to simplify matters. The opportunity was taken at its following General, at Brighton in 1945, to restore the status quo.

Snowploughs

Right at the end of their days 30530-30532, 30535, 30536, 30541-30543, 30545 and 30548, half of the class, were adapted to take snowploughs. The BR9637 forms listed the details in various ways as follows:

'Attachment for snowplough' 30530 12/62, 30531 11/62, 30532 12/62, 30536 12/62, 30542 11/62, 30548 1/62.

'Snowplough details fitted' 30541 2/63.

'Snowplough details marked off' 30535 12/63, 30545 1/64.

'Snowplough fitted' 30543 11/62.

With work for the engines very much on the wane it was obviously decided that they could serve as a 'standard plough' and when the dread winter of 1962-1963 is recalled we can only marvel at the prescience of the Southern Region authorities. An example of weather prediction never since equalled.

Lamp Brackets

The disposition was typically SR, one bracket top of the smokebox door, one left-hand side, one the right-hand side and three, as usual spread along the front buffer beam. There was the

same pattern on the back of the tender to facilitate working in reverse .

Snifting Valves

Snifting valves disappeared from the smokeboxes of Southern engines after the War. Prominent either side of the chimney, just as in other Southern classes with the Maunsell superheater, from 1946 they were deemed not to warrant the maintenance time and money involved and their general removal from Southern engines got underway. The process, according to Tibble (*The Southern Railway Q Class 0-6-0s, British Railways Illustrated Summer Special No.6*, Irwell Press 1998) had begun earlier on the Qs, in 1940; the valves allowed air to be drawn into the cylinders when coasting, avoiding problems of partial vacuum which inhibited running and the drawing in of ash which could cause damage. The regulator of 530 was altered in April 1940 to allow air to pass through during coasting and the snifters removed. 531 followed similarly in November 1940 but both had the valves refitted in 1943. The efficacy of the modification had been decided on but general application was postponed, put off till after the war's end. In spring 1946 as a general Southern-wide 'purge' of the valves got underway, those on 549 were

blanked off and the rest of the Qs followed in due course.

AWS

From the beginning of 1960 the Qs began to get the Automatic Warning System then being fitted across BR; the battery box was prominent, positioned lengthwise, on the left-hand running plate. In some instances it is recorded as 'BR ATC' – Automatic Train Control but it is the same thing. The programme was complete by 1962 with the exception of 30537.

TO WORK

The first, 530, went into traffic on 10 January 1938, running in traditionally out of Eastleigh. *The Railway Observer* gives a bit more detail: *530 is stationed at Eastleigh for the purpose of making trial workings between there and the Guildford district. They are comparatively small engines, intended for use throughout the system, where heavier types are not permitted or where power is at present being used unnecessarily. It is interesting to observe that they are the first 0-6-0s to be built by the Southern company itself. Further observations regarding this locomotive are as follows: It was noted at Bournemouth on Monday, 14th February, bearing Duty Board No.125, and again on 23rd February. It was then working the 1.20 (approx.) up*

If ever there was a chimney that merited the term 'mortification'… This is 30549 with its inner sleeve (not even a chimney proper) which nevertheless improved steaming. In fact thousands of steam locos across BR would have derived great advantage from such simple draughting proportion amendments but it was all too late to bother with. A few Qs were altered but that was it. Unfeasibly clean 30549 with its 'spout', is at Selsdon on 7 July 1961, standing in the goods yard to the east of the station, out of sight off to the right. A.W. Durrant, courtesy Richard Vitler.

goods, which is one of the Eastleigh 'running in' turns. On 22/2/38 it was observed on a special goods train from Southampton to Basingstoke. The load was thirty wagons and a brake van.

Early workings for 530 included the 8.35am Eastleigh to Alton goods, though normally loads could be quite light so '…no very severe test was imposed.'

From new they were on the South Western section, based at Eastleigh, Bournemouth, Nine Elms and Guildford – from the latter they ranged far to the east. On its first day of working the second loco, 531, worked the 9pm goods to Salisbury with over sixty wagons. In an unlikely running-in duty on 2 November 1938 537 spent all day as official works shunter at Eastleigh and this job probably went on for longer than that. Easter Monday the following year saw the same loco with a train formed of nine LNER coaches from Poole-Brighton while 538, also working from Poole, had ten coaches to Portsmouth. The Qs were regulars on excursions right through to the 1960s and operated in effect as mixed traffic engines, exactly as indicated by the *Southern Railway Magazine.*

Before the Second World War brought recording largely to an end, the entire Guildford allocation, 540-544, were noted on 20 May 1939 in use; 540 working passenger turns on the old SER line between Reading and Redhill, 541-543 on goods and 544 on shed ready to go. It had been reported that 545-549 were destined for Guildford shed but in fact the last five went new to Nine Elms. 545 did indeed arrive new to Guildford shed on 22 June 1939 only to be transferred to Nine Elms the very next day.

From new they were tried out on trains on the main line which were often a bit beyond the capability of such an 0-6-0, but the sheds threw them into the fray regardless. Strangely the war came to their 'rescue' with all the extra slow goods work coming their way. Traditional peacetime weekend excursions were no more. Duties included the evacuations of children from London and they played a part in Operation Dynamo following Dunkirk.
Allocation October 1939
Eastleigh 530, 532-539
Bournemouth 531
Guildford 540-544
Nine Elms 545-549

The class could be spared the more exacting duties when the Bulleid Q1s were introduced in 1942 and some were transferred to Horsham and Redhill. Thus the Central Section saw the class working a number of passenger duties on a regular basis, with appearances at London Bridge, Brighton, Eastbourne and Ashford and even further afield.

At November 1945 the Qs were disposed thus:
Bournemouth 548, 549
Eastleigh 530, 532, 539, 547
Guildford 545, 546
Horsham 540-544
Redhill 531, 533-538

There were further main line London workings, following the path earlier beaten by those at Redhill and Horsham. Bradley outlines the background in *Locomotives of the Southern Railway Part 1* – post-war, such Central Section London steam passenger services were in the hands of a motley collection of pre-Group I3 4-4-2Ts, 4-4-0s and even H 0-4-4Ts. High mileage 543, so worse for wear that several days had to be spent getting it fighting fit, was dispatched from Horsham (where it was presumably the worst of the five Qs there) to Tunbridge Wells West. The stage was set for the spectacle in April 1947 of 543 at the head of an afternoon Victoria-Eastbourne four coach relief. Permanent transfers to Tunbridge Wells West for this work followed late in 1947 and in 1948 and they also appeared at Three bridges, which also brought them to London on passenger work. They were, to repeat a point made earlier, genuinely mixed traffic locomotives, with a range of duties possibly wider than any other comparable group of 0-6-0s in the country.

Allocation June 1948 (BR numbers)
Bournemouth 30548, 30549
Eastleigh 30530, 30532, 30535, 30536
Horsham 30545, 30546
Redhill 30533, 30537, 30538, 30539
Three Bridges 30540, 30541, 30547
Tunbridge Wells West 30531, 30534, 30542, 30543, 30544

After inevitable reshufflings, the position at 21 May 1949 was:
Bournemouth 30548, 30549
Eastleigh 30530, 30532, 30535, 30536
Horsham 30531, 30545, 30546
Three Bridges 30540, 30541
Tunbridge Wells West 30534, 30542, 30543, 30544

Norwood Junction 30533, 30537, 30538, 30539, 30547

By now the Qs were perhaps beginning to look a bit more like goods engines. The Redhill ones had been displaced by K 2-6-0s and in 1950 ten Fairburn LM 2-6-4Ts built at Brighton went new to Tunbridge Wells West for passenger work. From hereon the 0-6-0s were rostered more to goods work but could still shine on excursions, some of them of prodigious length. The summer of 1950 saw the Bournemouth and Eastleigh ones on specials, often of ten coaches, on the Swanage branch.

Allocation 1 January 1952
Bournemouth 30548, 30549
Eastleigh 30530, 30531, 30532, 30535, 30536, 30542, 30543, 30544
Horsham 30545, 30546
Norwood Junction 30533, 30534, 30537, 30538, 30539, 30547
Three Bridges 30540, 30541

On 5 June 1952 main line diesel 10201 caught fire while working the down Royal Wessex and was stopped at Beaulieu Road where the fire brigade was called. 30548 on the following 6.07pm from Southampton Terminus pushed the train and diesel to Brockenhurst as well as pulling its

own train. Here the train was taken on by Q1 33024 and T9 30285. This was an even more extraordinary cavalcade, assuming it still included 10201.

The Qs were in a sense 'weekend engines' pressed into service throughout the summer; in 1954 for instance a regular summer Sunday Victoria-Sheerness excursion was rostered to a Norwood Junction Q, timed to depart London at 10.50am, though the times changed over the years. On 20 June yet another Sunday excursion was noted, from Carshalton to Margate double headed by 30534 and 30537.

Allocation 1 January 1956
Bournemouth 30539 30541 30548
Eastleigh 30530, 30531, 30532, 30535, 30536, 30542, 30543
Horsham 30544, 30545, 30546, 30547
Norwood Junction 30533, 30534, 30537, 30538, 30540, 30549

The class was now grouped on four sheds and 30549 had certainly travelled from its old Wessex haunts when on 19 June 1956 it was observed on a goods train at Folkestone Junction. There were still instances (these probably finally ended about 1960) of Qs working passenger trains into Victoria; 30537 for instance on 14

Qs on trains 1. Bournemouth's 30548 with a freight coming off the 'old road' at Brockenhurst about 1962.

During the winter of 1960 Norwood Junction had two duties listed for its Qs…
Duty 581.
Loco departed from the shed at 3.30am, running light to Norwood yard, leaving the yard at 4am, working a goods train to Reigate, arriving at 5.15am.
Departed at 6.30am working a goods to Guildford and arriving at 10.30am, departing at 11.33am to Shalford, arrived there at 11.45am. Shunted here between 11.50am to 12.15pm and departed with a goods at 12.20pm back to Guildford, arriving at 12.36pm. Light engine to Guildford shed for servicing and turning.
2pm ran light engine to Woking, arrived at 2.20pm and departed on a goods train to Redhill, due to arrive there at 4.09pm.
Light engine to Loco yard, staying there until 9.45pm.
Worked to Redhill Up yard and departed at 10.05pm on goods train to Norwood Yard due at 11.05pm.
Light engine back to Norwood shed.
'Redhill men work round to Reigate where they were relieved by Guildford men at 6.09am. Guildford men worked the engine until the return from Woking where they dispose the engine and home passenger on the 5.31pm to Guildford. Redhill worked the 9.45pm departure off shed and finished the duty.'

Duty 582.
Loco departed the shed at 4.50am and arrived at Norwood yard. Departed on a goods train at 5.20am to Groombridge, arrived at 8.35am. Light engine to Tunbridge Wells West shed at 9.08am arrived at 9.14am.
Day was spent at Tunbridge Wells West, departed at 4.55pm, light engine to station to shunt stock between 5pm and 5.20pm then worked the 5.29pm passenger to Ashurst and departed there at 6.08pm, arrived at Tunbridge Wells West at 6.19pm.
6.40pm departed light engine to Crowborough, arrived at 7pm. Departed here at 7.17pm on goods train to Norwood yard, arrived at 9.52pm, then light engine to Norwood shed.
'Norwood men worked round to Tunbridge Wells West and left the loco on shed. Here it was prepared by Tunbridge Wells West men for the light engine movement at 4.55pm. Norwood men took over at 5.20pm and finished the duty.'

At the same time Three Bridges shed had this duty for a Q.
Duty 690.
Departed light engine from shed at 6.30pm to Three Bridges A.N.R. (Assistance Not Required) With loco from duty no.531 off Bricklayers Arms shed.
Goods to Norwood No.1 Up Goods, arrived at 12.58am.
Departed at 1.20am with a goods, arrived at New Cross Gate at 1.42am. Shunted here between 3.15 and 4.15am; departed New Cross Gate at 4.35pm on goods train and arrived at Three Bridges yard at 5.58am.
Light engine at 6.10am to Horsham, arrived at 6.35am.
Shunted here between 6.55 and 8.20am, departed on a goods at 8.33am.
Arrived at Littlehampton at 11.27am. Shunted here between 11.30am and 2.15pm. Departed on goods at 2.35pm to Chichester, arrived at 3.33pm, departed on goods at 4.34pm to Barnham, arrived at 4.48pm. Back to Chichester at 5.32pm, arrived at 5.47pm.
Finally departed Chichester at 7.27pm on a van train to Horsham, arrived 9.28pm. Light engine at 9.30pm to arrive back on shed at 9.54pm.
'Three Bridges had the work round to Horsham at 6.35am. Loco double headed the 12.03am night goods from Three Bridges to Norwood No.1 Up Goods with loco off duty no.531 off Bricklayers Arms shed, normally a West Country class. Horsham men came onto the loco at 6.35am. Relieved by Bognor men at Arundel at 10.54am. In turn relieved by Horsham men at Barnham at 5.02pm. Three Bridges men came on at 7.45pm at Barnham and completed the duty.'

August 1958, on the 5.47pm Tunbridge Wells West to Victoria.

On 9 May 1959 it was the turn of Horsham's 30544 to find itself at Folkestone Junction, having worked the 1.17pm from Ashford: *…an unusual sight, engines of this type have lately been noted on the 10.46am Queenborough to Bricklayers Arms goods; on Whit Sunday 30545 was noted on the 10.46am Victoria to Sheerness via Nunhead and Chatham and on the afternoon of May 24th 30534 hauled empty stock through Margate, later proceeding to Ramsgate shed.*

Allocation 1 January 1960
Bournemouth 30539, 30541, 30548
Eastleigh 30530, 30531, 30532, 30535, 30536, 30542, 30543
Norwood Junction 30533, 30534, 30537, 30538, 30540, 30549
Three Bridges 30544-30547

Horsham shed had lost its independent existence in July 1959 and became in effect a sub-shed of its own former outstation, Three Bridges, with locos henceforward listed under the latter, coded 75E.

On 30 April 1960 30543 was at Fareham on the Portsmouth portion of the 1pm from Cardiff and a Q still had a Victoria connection – during May the 4.48pm from Victoria would split at Ashurst with a U1 leaving on the Brighton portion and a Q taking the rear four coaches to Tunbridge Wells West. Whitsun was a principal holiday during these times and on Whit Sunday 1960 30544 was on a day excursion to Brighton from Reading which ran via the Horsham to Guildford line.

1961 was the last full year of the class, withdrawals getting underway in the summer of 1962. It was also the first

year that Brighton got some of them; the first two to arrive were 30533 and 30538 in March, joined at various times by 30531, 30534, 30535, 30537, 30543, 30544 and 30549, mainly from Norwood Junction.

Allocation 5 January 1962
Brighton 30533-30535, 30537, 30538, 30544, 30549
Bournemouth 30539, 30541 30548
Eastleigh 30530-30532, 30536, 30542, 30543
Three Bridges 30540, 30545-30547

In August 1962 came a surprise from *Modern Railways: Stewarts Lane becomes a Central Division depot, recoded 75D and amongst its new acquisitions are four class Q 0-6-0s from Brighton which have evidently taken the place of withdrawn class C 0-6-0s.* The four Qs were 30537 30538 30544 and 30549.

At the end of 1962 30530 and 30531 were moved to Exmouth Junction, the only two of the class ever based there. Their purpose was to replace class 700 0-6-0s on snowplough duties, 'as required'. Both were transferred away in July 1963. The late transformation of the Qs into snowploughs is described earlier in the text.

30531 and 30543 contributed to the LCGB 'Hayling Farewell' on 3 November 1963 when 30531 and 30543 double headed Havant to Chichester to Lavant to Horsham to Three Bridges and up to Victoria. By the end of 1964 only three survived, 30535, 30545 and 30548 all adapted for snowplough work; 30548 was the last one active, in March 1965, eking out its time at Eastleigh on local goods. Happily 541 survives on the Bluebell Railway in Sussex.

Amid the weeds at Redhill on 5 July 1964; officially withdrawn a fortnight later, 30531 is surely out of use by now but it still provides a good illustration of several features. Underneath the smokebox door on the flat-fronted Qs were two removable plates, each with two handles. The plates could be unbolted for access to the cylinder heads and the handles were there to remove them once they were unbolted. The little domes cover the piston valve tail rods. 30531 has AWS of course; the battery box is mounted sideways on the running plate while the unit mounted behind, on the cab front, is the AWS relay box. Just visible in outline directly under the near buffer is the AWS receiver – something hardly ever visible in photographs. The AWS conduit runs along the valence and loops down in front of the sandbox. As mentioned elsewhere, the Qs did not have the familiar protection plate usually mounted below the buffer beam on AWS-fitted engines. The steam reverser is prominent as ever, the locking cylinder to the front, operating cylinder behind. The big pipe running along the boiler is the vacuum ejector and the rodding with its right-angle between the front sandbox and the buffer beam works the cylinder drain cock gear. Peter Groom.

Top left. Qs on trains 2. 30545 at St Mary Cray Junction with a substantial train on 18 May 1959. Mike King writes: *Interesting this one. Not sure about a regular working and I am not certain that 30545 was ever a SE section loco. I recall it at Redhill, Three Bridges and finally at Nine Elms. The headcode is Victoria to Dover via Chatham, which isn't much help. The set is Maunsell special traffic set 456, formed of brake seconds 4083 and 4084, composites 5694 and 5610 (the second and third vehicles) followed by four unclassed open saloons, nos.4394, 7965, 7968 and 7975 with a loose coach on the rear. I am guessing empty stock of some sort. The period is just before the start of electrification of the North Kent route to Dover; it was a Monday so the train may be return empties after a weekend excursion. It would not be Whit Monday, as that was likely to be one or two weeks later. Whatever the precise circumstances, it was just the sort of job a Q might find itself on.* RailOnline

Above. Qs on trains 3. The Qs could be found on substantial passenger loadings more or less to their final years, which surely marks them out from any comparable 0-6-0. Particularly notable 'last hurrahs' concerned the packed and lengthy Saturday trains on the Lymington Pier branch. Proving it still packs a mixed traffic (or 'General utility' as the Southern Railway put it) punch is Eastleigh's 30543 at Lymington Junction with an up working to Waterloo as far as Bournemouth, 28 July 1962. RailOnline

Left. The most obvious detail of the Q 0-6-0s was the steam reverser on the left-hand side and its various feeds and pipes. All steam reversers have two cylinders. The rearward one is the steam cylinder that actually operates the gear while the other one, forward of it, provides the hydraulic 'lock' so that, in theory, the gear stays where the driver wants it. Note the piston rod emerging from the latter to its attachment to the reversing shaft. All the various designs however, suffered from 'creep' to some degree or other and the Q1s and Bulleid Pacifics which also had the gear were notorious for this. Of the latter, those not rebuilt are still so fitted and still experience 'creep'. Sometimes the gear will go from wherever it was set to full gear, with disastrous results for the poor fireman!

The Record

Abbreviations for Southern Railway repairs:
A = General
B = Intermediate
C = Casual
D = Non-classified

The following codes were used for repairs under British Railways, based on LMS practice.
GO = General Overhaul
HC = Heavy Casual
HI = Heavy Intermediate
LC = Light Casual
LI = Light Intermediate
Int = Intermediate
NC = Non-classified
Some were upgraded as the work unfolded such as LI-HI but downgrading, as in LC-NC for instance, seldom occurred. Repairs were normally dealt with at Eastleigh Works.

'Return' or 'Defect' indicates a return visit to works normally soon after a classified repair to rectify (on the LMS for instance it was called 'Rectification') a problem often found during running-in trials.

The collection of *BR Southern Region: Form BR 9637: Return of Locomotives undergoing or awaiting repairs at...Locomotive Works: Week ending* held at the National Archive lists numerous 'Locomotive Alterations' in the latter part of the 1950s and into the early 1960s, almost all fairly minor and invisible to the observer – the most notable for our purposes is the entry for AWS/ATC gear. Other entries include:
Spark arrester gear*
Blowdown gear and silencer, Briquette tube feeder.
Split pins and collars to regulator pins in place of circlips, or
Split pins to regulator link pins in place of circlips.
Vacuum exhaust pipe drain and elbow.

One entry only applied to two of the class – the front buffer beams of 30536 and 30547 required 'strengthened gussets' presumably as a result of corrosion:
30536 13/6/61-29/7/61**GO**
30547 27/9/61-28/10/61**GO**

In reality smokebox self-cleaning screens.

30544 at Eastleigh on 21 October 1950; it would have acquired the large first emblem not long before. H.C. Casserley, courtesy M. Casserley.

30530 at Nine Elms on 17 July 1964, now fitted with modified frames which have been given lifting holes. AWS battery box, relay box above this side, with piping running under the valence. Peter Groom.

30530

To traffic as 530 10/1/38
Renumbered 30530 24/2/50

Works

19/3/40-24/4/40**B**	56,647
	Snifting valves removed 12 new small tubes 'Howell'
28/5/43-7/7/43**A**	141,644
	Snifting valves refitted 100 copper stays & 320 monel metal stays riveted over 320 nuts renewed Copper tube rivets & seams caulked 2 new fusible plugs 158 new small tubes 'Howell' 21 new superheater tubes
15/12/44-29/1/45**C**	41,866 Eastleigh shed
	158 new small tubes
20/12/46-18/1/47**A**	89,907
	136 copper & 186 monel metal stays renewed 100 monel metal stays caulked 100 nuts renewed 40 roof stays renewed 4 holes bushed Copper firebox flanges welded 158 new small tubes 'Howell' Set new superheater tubes Lemaitre blastpipe large diameter chimney
3/9/48-25/9/48**LI**	34,103
	100 copper stays riveted over 150 monel steel stays caulked 2 new fusible plugs 158 new small tubes 'Talbot & Stead ' 21 new superheater tubes
25/1/50-24/2/50**GO**	66,108
	Renumbered 30530 6 copper stays & 32 monel stays renewed 280 nuts renewed Copper firehole lap welded Firehole 16 new rivets 158 new small tubes 'Howell' 14 new & 7 second hand superheater tubes
18/8/52-12/9/52**GO**	New copper firebox New ½ steel Tube Plate Set of new small tubes & superheater tubes
14/9/53-26/9/53**LC**	
16/9/54-9/10/54**LI-HI**	50,433
	Tender doors & handrails modified to Drg.E46477 2 new fusible plugs 3 superheater tubes renewed 18 repaired 21 ferrules fitted
17/7/56-26/7/56**LC**	93,482
	96 monel metals stays repaired 2 new fusible plugs Set new small tubes 'Stewart & Lloyds'
14/12/56-22/12/56**LC**	102,193
10/1/58-8/2/58**GO**	126,070
	347 monel metal stays & 547 nuts renewed 2 new fusible plugs Firehole 84 rivets recaulked 158 new small tubes 'Stewart & Lloyds' 21 new superheater tubes
3/6/58-14/6/58**LC**	7,727
23/6/60-9/7/60**LI**	47,961
	AWS Blowdown equipment Briquette tube feeder Vacuum exhaust drain pipe Split pin to regulator link pins in place of circlips 10 copper & 390 monel metal stays riveted over 390 nuts renewed 2 new fusible plugs Foundation Ring 32 rivets repaired 30 second hand small tubes Frames modified
22/9/61-7/10/61**LC**	73,862
	Spark arrester gear BR class 4 chimney & blastpipe
31/7/62-18/8/62**LC**	85,865
	100 monel metal stays riveted over 100 nuts renewed 2 new fusible plugs 158 new small tubes 'Stewart & Lloyds' 15 new superheater tubes
7/12/62-8/12/62**NC**	87,435
	Attachment for snow plough

Boilers

No.1064	from new
No.1071	7/7/43
No.1075	18/1/47
No.1079	24/2/50
No.1066	12/9/52
No.1072	8/2/58

Tender

No.1904	from new

Sheds

Eastleigh	8/1/38
Exmouth Jct	17/12/62
Bournemouth	22/7/63
Nine Elms	6/1/64

Withdrawn 20/12/64 Nine Elms shed.

30530 at the Eastleigh coal stage, 9 July 1949; Bulleid multi-blastpipe chimney, snifting valves still there but with none of the piping forward to the smokebox front which can be observed on the engines before the War. Tender bare at this point. 530 went new to Eastleigh (it remained allocated there till 1962) and *The Railway Observer* at the time noted: *Class Q 530 has been at Bournemouth from Eastleigh and now works on the Swanage branch on Saturdays. It is nearly always on the 9.20am train from Swanage, and on the 1.55 London train. This is believed to be the first SR standard type to work on the Swanage branch, also the largest type.* H.C. Casserley, courtesy M. Casserley.

30530 now with BR chimney at Eastleigh shed on 31 August 1962; this was the first one and the only one with the angular frames at the front, as noted earlier. Patch welded repair on tender 'rave'. The Qs, curiously, did not have the protecting 'bash plate' which prevented the coupling swinging back and damaging the AWS. Presumably it was positioned sufficiently out of the way to obviate this fitting. The absence of the plate means it is not obvious if an engine has AWS or not, at least from this side. The armoured cable looping behind the right-hand (far) buffer is the clue. Peter Groom.

30531

To traffic as 531 8/6/38
Renumbered 30531 15/1/49

Works

19/8/40-6/11/40**B**	58,139
	Lemaitre blastpipe, large diameter chimney Snifting valves removed Extension of mileage 10,000 100 copper & 50 monel metal stays renewed 600 monel metal stays riveted over & 600 nuts renewed 158 new small tubes 'Tubes Ltd' Superheater tubes expanded
11/4/41-4/6/41**C**	66,719
1/9/43-13/10/43**A**	117,032 Snifting valves refitted Collgraf colloidal graphite lubrication fitted 30 steel stays renewed & 400 riveted over 400 nuts renewed 30 holes bushed 158 new small tubes 21 second hand superheater tubes
3/1/45-26/2/45**C**	31,324 Bricklayers Arms
	Collgraf lubrication removed 158 new small tubes
5/6/46-11/6/46**D**	61,442 Stewarts Lane
6/2/47-16/2/47**D**	72,381 Ashford
26/9/47-18/12/47**C**	80,502 New Cross Gate
	Wasted stay nuts in Fire area removed Rivets in tube plate & back plate flanges drilled & caulked Small tubes expanded & beaded to tube plate
15/3/48-17/4/48**B**	80,609
	Extension of mileage 10,000 178 copper & 166 monel metal stays renewed 170 monel metal stays riveted over 2 angle patches on back plate 2 new fusible plugs 158 new small tubes 'Howell' Set second hand superheater tubes
13/12/48-15/1/49**C**	90,303
	Renumbered 30531
22/5/50-29/6/50**A**	116,580
	120 new monel metal stays & 200 repaired 320 nuts renewed Internal tube plate flanges repaired with studs Set new small tubes Superheater tubes ferrules renewed
26/11/52-24/12/52**GO**	58,256
	210 monel metal stays & 310 nuts renewed All roof stays renewed 158 new small tubes 'Howell' 21 new superheater tubes
7/5/53-16/5/53**return**	7,790
	20 copper stays renewed Copper tube 2 angle patches
23/12/54-15/1/55**LI-HI**	46,423
	Tender doors & handrails modified to Drg.E46477 88 monel metal stays riveted over & 88 nuts renewed 2 new fusible plugs 158 new small tubes 'Howell' 21 new superheater tubes
28/5/56-9/6/56**LC**	84,918
	10 copper stays renewed 140 monel metal stays riveted over & 150 nuts renewed 2 new fusible plugs 158 new small tubes 'Stewart & Lloyds' 3 new superheater tubes
17/7/56-21/7/56**LC**	86,121
24/8/56-1/9/56**LC**	86,177
	25 monel metal stays riveted over & 25 nuts renewed 2 new fusible plugs 125 new small tubes 'Stewart & Lloyds' 19 new superheater tubes
7/5/57-25/5/57**GO**	114,723
12/2/59-7/3/59**LI-HI**	44,990
15/11/61-9/12/61**LC**	101,017
	AWS Spark arrester gear
11/4/62-19/5/62**GO**	105,483
	Blowdown gear & silencer Briquette tube feeder 1096 monel metal stays & 1096 nuts renewed All tubeplate & roof stays renewed 250 holes bushed New copper firebox 158 new small tubes 'Stewart & Lloyds' 21 new superheater tubes
19/6/62-23/6/62**LC**	60,497
26/11/62-27/11/62**NC**	67,488
	Attachment for snow plough

Boilers

No.1065	from new
No.1083	13/10/43
No.1078	17/4/48
No.1077	29/6/50
No.1079	24/12/52
No.1080	25/5/57
No.1073	19/5/62

Tender

No.1901	from new

Sheds

Bournemouth	11/7/38
Redhill	by 1942
Tunbridge W W	27/12/47
Horsham	31/5/48
Eastleigh	9/9/50
Exmouth Jct	17/12/62
Three Bridges	22/7/63
Brighton	6/1/64
Redhill	25/5/64

Withdrawn 19/7/64 Redhill shed.

30531, an Eastleigh engine for all of the 1950s, shunts its train on Southampton Town Quay on 11 August 1955. 531 used 'Collgraf Colloidal Graphite Lubrication' in an experiment during the War (surprisingly) in 1943. The makers claimed it offered more reliable delivery of the lubricant but no obvious advantage was noted. During a visit to Bricklayers Arms shops over January-February 1945 it was removed and the original system put back on. Tony Wright.

30531 at Eastleigh MPD. The date is not known but it is likely to be after the loco's General completed in May 1957; newly applied (large) second emblem, 4F above number and water treatment triangle below (it was a circle at first – see earlier) but changed because it was confused with the WR route restriction disk. ColourRail

30532

To traffic as 532 15/6/38
Renumbered 30532 2/12/50

Works

20/5/39**D**		
15/1/41-12/3/41**A**	67,304	

2 new fusible plugs 158 second hand small tubes welded

29/12/43-19/1/44**A**	77,083	

58 copper stays renewed Rivets and seams caulked 2 new fusible plugs

26/3/46-18/4/46**B**	62,928	

Extension of mileage 5,000 91 copper stays renewed Copper tube 4 flanges welded studs caulked 2 new fusible plugs Test No.1941 Engine cylinder oil Test still in operation 20/4/46

30/5/47-28/6/47**A**	86,467	

Lemaitre blastpipe large diameter chimney 609 monel metal stays riveted over & 80 repaired 130 holes bushed New tube plate & ½ sides

11/1/49-12/2/49**LC**	33,850	Eastleigh shed

Set new superheater tubes

7/11/50-2/12/50**LI**	78,227	

Renumbered 30532 300 monel metal stays repaired Tube & fire hole plates to be studded & caulked 2 new fusible plugs Set new small tubes and set new superheater tubes

21/10/52-22/11/52**GO**	125,159	
7/9/54-8/10/54**LC**	38,776 Eastleigh shed	
20/5/55-3/6/55**LI**	53,770	

Cab doors & handrails on tender no.1900 modified to Drg.E46477

2/5/56-16/5/56**LC**	78,392	
11/6/57-6/7/57**GO**	103,487	

54 monel metal stays & 470 nuts renewed Copper tube 2 copper angles fitted Copper wrapping 2 flat patches fitted 2 new fusible plugs 2 fusible plug holes bushed for re-allocation of plugs 158 new small tubes 'Stewart & Lloyds' Set new superheater tubes

28/5/59-13/6/59**LI**	46,642	

Collars & split pins fitted to regulator link in place of circlips 330 steel stays riveted over 30 monel metal nuts repaired Foundation ring 32 rivets repaired 30 new small tubes 'Stewart & Lloyds' 3 new superheater tubes

12/11/59-21/11/59**NC**	52,271	

1 monel metal stay renewed Copper tube welded Foundation ring 12 rivets repaired

7/4/61-6/5/61**GO**	84,449	

232 monel metal stays & 360 nuts renewed Copper tube 26 studs renewed 2 new fusible plugs Foundation ring 14 new rivets 158 new small tubes 'Stewart & Lloyds' 21 new superheater tubes AWS by 1961

4/12/62-5/12/62**NC**	30,602	

Snow plough attachment

Boilers

No.1066	from new
No.1064	19/1/44
No.1081	18/4/46
No.1072	28/6/47
No.1067	22/11/52
No.1073	6/7/57
No.1075	6/5/61

Tender

No.1900	from new

Sheds

Eastleigh 11/7/38
Redhill by 1942
Eastleigh by 5/1945
Salisbury 17/12/62

Withdrawn 5/1/64 Salisbury shed.

A filthy 30532 at Eastleigh in the 1950s. D. Preston, ColourRail

There is no mistake about the level of this overhaul. With a full glistening repaint this is after 30532's General of 1961, attention which would see it through to withdrawal early in 1964. ColourRail

30532 after repair at Eastleigh. The date is not known but might be after its Light Intermediate of 1959. Wheels, motion, axleboxes, smokebox, buffer beam have all received attention but there has been no repaint. Note not often seen right-facing lion in crest. Norman Preedy..

30533

To traffic as 533 July 1938
Renumbered 30533 no date

Works

19/7/47-2/8/47		Lemaitre blastpipe, large diameter chimney 100 copper & 500 steel stays riveted over 500 nuts renewed 2 fusible plugs& brick arch studs renewed 158 new small tubes
2/9/49		71 copper & 177 monel metal stays new 20 roof stays renewed Copper firehole flanges& firehole welded 2 new fusible plugs
7/3/52		301 monel metal stays renewed All roof stays renewed New back plate Wrapper studs renewed & plate welded Set new small tubes & new superheater tubes
26/3/54-24/4/54**LI-HI**	40,511	Cab tender sides and hand rails modified 220 monel metal stays repaired 220 nuts renewed Copper tube & copper firehole flanges repaired 2 new fusible plugs Barrel ring caulked Set new small tubes & new superheater tubes 2 fusible plug holes bushed for re-allocation of plugs
26/4/57-8/6/57**GO**	101,477	All monel metal stays roof stays & nuts renewed New copper firebox 158 new small tubes 'Stewart & Lloyds' 21 new superheater tubes
11/12/59-9/1/60**LI**	49,750	BR type ATC fitted 345 monel metal stays riveted over 360 nuts renewed 2 new fusible plugs Foundation ring 4 rivets repaired 158 new small tubes 'Stewart & Lloyds' 5 new superheater tubes
11/1/63-12/1/63**NC**	Eastleigh shed	

Boilers

No.1081	2/8/47
No.1076	2/9/49
No.1073	7/3/52
No.1082	8/6/57

Tenders

No.1907	from new
No.1906	no date

Sheds

Eastleigh	11/7/38
Redhill	by 1942
Norwood Jct	31/7/48
Brighton	18/3/61
Stewarts Lane	19/11/62
Bournemouth	30/12/62

Withdrawn 30/3/63 Bournemouth shed.

533 (snifting valves still in place) at Norwood Junction in 1949, accompanying one of the Westinghouse WD 2-8-0s still on the Southern. transporttreasury

30533 undergoing attention at Norwood Junction The date is not known and the 75C Norwood Junction shedplate is no help, the engine being there through the entirety of the 1950s though it would be prior to its General of 1957, when the small first emblem would give way to the second version. Triangle water treatment symbol below number, but no 4F above yet. D. Preston, ColourRail

Fine detail on 30533 (a plated 'rave' on the tender this side) in the yard at Eastleigh MPD, 5 April 1963. It had been at Brighton since March 1961 and it still bears the 75A shed plate despite transfers since November 1962 (to Stewarts Lane) and then Bournemouth a few weeks later before withdrawal in March 1963. By this time it was hardly worth the bother of swapping such plates. Peter Groom.

Second emblem now, in an unlikely combination at Hampden Park, just outside Eastbourne. The train has come from Tunbridge Wells West via the Cuckoo line and the Q (with burnt smokebox door) has been attached to the 2-6-4T en route to get to Eastbourne shed. It was a regular double headed working. Norman Preedy.

30534

To traffic as 534 31/8/38
Renumbered 30534 17/6/48

Works

5/3/41-16/4/41**A**	70,371	
	2 new fusible plugs 158 second hand small tubes welded Superheater tubes expanded & referruled	
29/11/43-29/12/43**A**	76,212	
	Rivets and seams caulked 2 fusible plugs 158 second hand small tubes	
7/11/45-15/12/45**C**	50,482 Ashford	
	100 coper stays riveted over 75 new nuts 158 new small tubes 'Talbot & Stead'	
6/6/46-22/6/46**C**	59,358	
	Lemaitre blastpipe large diameter chimney 54 stays caulked and 54 nuts renewed 2 new fusible plugs 158 new small tubes 'New Steel'	
2/6/47-2/7/47**A**	82,386	
	98 copper & 39 steel stays renewed 200 steel stays repaired All roof stays renewed Firehole welded 158 new small tubes 'Howell' 21 new superheater tubes	
14/6/48-17/6/48**D**	23,258 Brighton	
	Renumbered 30534	
24/5/49-31/5/49**D**	45,457 Nine Elms	
	80 steel stays riveted over 42 nuts renewed All tubes rebeaded & expanded 21 ferrules renewed	
8/11/49-21/12/49**LC**	55,338 Stewarts Lane	
	50 second hand small tubes 21 expanded	
5/12/50-30/12/50**A**	70,123	
	461 monel metal stays & 581 nuts renewed 195 holes bushed Copper tubes rivets replaced by studs 2 new fusible plugs Set new small tubes & superheater tubes	
10/10/52-31/10/52**LC**	41,006 Redhill	
	Set new small tubes 3 new superheater tubes	
24/9/53-11/11/53**HI**	59,584 Brighton	
29/4/55-21/5/55**GO**	93,150	
	30 monel metal & all roof stays renewed 2 fusible plugs Copper tube 2 angle patches Copper firehole 24 rivets renewed 158 new small tubes 'Howell' Set new superheater tubes	
28/1/57-27/2/57**LC**	34,881 Norwood Jct	
	158 new small tubes & 3 new superheater tubes	
31/10/57-23/11/57**LI-GO**	47,386	
	170 holes bushed New copper firebox Casing covering 2 ½ sides fitted & welded 158 new small tubes 'Stewart & Lloyds' 21 new superheater tubes	
19/5/60-4/6/60**LI**	44,159	
	AWS Regulator link pins fitted with split ins in place of circ clip 10 copper 355 monel metal stays riveted over & 370 nuts renewed 2 fusible plugs Copper tube seams & 48 studs repaired 2 new fusible plugs 158 new small tubes 'Stewart & Lloyds' 3 new superheater tubes	
10/10/62-26/10/62**LC**	85,219	
	Spark arrester gear	

Boilers

No.1068	from new
No.1065	29/12/43
No.1071	2/7/47
No.1078	30/12/50
No.1084	21/5/55
No.1079	23/11/57

Tender

No.1903	from new

Sheds

Eastleigh	20/8/38
Redhill	by 1942
Tunbridge W W	27/12/47
Norwood Jct	5/8/50
Brighton	3/5/61
Stewarts Lane	19/11/62

534 at Eastleigh on 15 October 1938. Allocated there from new, it would move to Redhill in the War and would stay allocated to the east thereafter. H.C. Casserley, courtesy M. Casserley.

Withdrawn 22/12/62 Stewarts Lane shed.

30534 at Tunbridge Wells West MPD, 16 March 1958. The shed and the station were intimately close, so that of these two tracks in this 'bay' at the west end, one belonged to the shed (hence 30534 being stabled thereon) and one to the station, the veranda and platform of which are visible at the right. The shed building and water tank are at the left; note the sign FIRELIGHTERS Smoking Prohibited, one of the few places you were *not* allowed to smoke in 1958! ColourRail

30534 at Norwood Junction MPD in November 1959, a few rogue whiffs of steam from the reverser cylinders. Peter Groom.

30535

To traffic as 535 7/9/38
Renumbered S535 31/1/48; 30535 6/11/48

Works

1/2/40-17/2/40**C**	35,886
5/12/40	Eastleigh shed
	Extension of mileage 10,000 158 new small tubes
18/7/41-3/9/41**A**	74,626
	10 second hand small tubes & welded
26/2/42-11/5/42**B**	7,942
18/3/44-26/4/44**C**	61,571 Bricklayers Arms
	158 small tubes second hand
18/10/44-24/11/44**A**	74,955 Ashford
	230 monel metal stays riveted over 230 nuts renewed 2 new fusible plugs 16 new small tubes 21 superheater tubes second hand
23/11/45-20/12/45**C**	25,998 Bricklayers Arms
22/1/47-24/2/47**C**	49,626 Eastleigh shed
	50 monel metal stays replaced by copper stays 2 new fusible plugs All small tubes renewed 'Talbot Stead' Set new superheater tubes
5/1/48-31/1/48**A**	63,895
	Renumbered S535 Lemaitre blastpipe large diameter chimney Set new crown stays 470 new monel metal stays & 100 repaired 150 holes bushed Firehole welded 2 new fusible plugs Set new small tubes 'Howell' Set new superheater tubes
27/10/48-6/11/48**C**	11,091
	Renumbered 30535 1 new copper & 26 new monel metals stays 250 monel metal stays repaired & 250 new nuts 20 holes bushed Plates seams rivets & studs repaired 2 new fusible plugs 36 small tubes expanded & rebeaded
11/5/49-13/5/49**D**	18,595
5/4/50-14/4/50**LC**	36,640
2/4/51-25/4/51**HI**	54,774
	3 new copper & 3 new monel metal stays 250 monel metal stays repaired 2 new fusible plugs Set new small tubes & superheater tubes
14/9/53-8/10/53**GO**	115,076
	53 copper 683 monel metal & 20 roof stays stays renewed New copper back plate 2 new fusible plugs Set new small tubes & superheater tubes
4/8/55-27/8/55**LI-HI**	46,678
	80 copper & 260 monel metal stays riveted over 260 nuts & 140 roof stays renewed 2 new fusible plugs Set new small tubes 'Stewart & Lloyds' Set new superheater tubes
15/8/56-15/9/56**LC**	73,195
	LC-HC Cancelled ref. CM&EE [Shopping Bureau]
29/3/57-8/4/57**NC-LC**	85,215
	6 second hand small tubes
9/9/57-28/9/57**LI-HI**	95,823
	306 monel metal stays repaired & 2 steel stays renewed 980 copper stays riveted over 306 nuts renewed 2 new fusible plugs Barrel ring caulked Firehole top welded Firehole 15 rivets renewed 158 second small tubes 21 new superheater tubes
15/4/58-26/4/58**LC**	110,395
21/5/59-13/6/59**GO**	137,452
	Collars & split pins fitted to regulator link in place of Cir clips All monel metal stays nuts & all roof stays renewed New firebox 158 new small tubes 'Universal' 21 new superheater tubes
23/5/61-3/6/61**NC-LC**	41,689
	AWS gear Strengthening gussets to front buffer beam
30/7/62-25/8/62**HI**	61,146
	320 monel metal stays riveted over 320 nuts renewed 2 new fusible plugs Foundation Ring 28 rivets recaulked 158 new small tubes 'Stewart & Lloyds' 21 new superheater tubes
17/12/63-20/12/63**NC**	84,144
	Snowplough details marked off

Boilers

No.1069	from new
No.1070	31/1/48
No.1083	8/10/53
No.1069	13/6/59

Tender

No.1905	from new

Sheds

Eastleigh	17/9/38
Redhill	by 1942
Eastleigh	15/6/46
Brighton	6/7/61
Stewarts Lane	19/11/62
Bournemouth	17/12/62
Salisbury	6/1/64
Guildford	18/1/65

Withdrawn 25/4/65 Guildford shed.

535 new at Eastleigh shed, 15 October 1938; in view are a cast number plate, a serif SOUTHERN, a block 535 and, on the tender rear, a *shaded* serif number – see also pages 4-5. H.C. Casserley, courtesy M. Casserley.

30535 with a down freight near Sway on 2 May 1963 – a reminder of what an 0-6-0 in the upper reaches of the 4F power classification could do. One would hardly think, looking at his scene, that the same engines could rush commuters down from town to Tunbridge Wells, or excursionists to the seaside. transporttreasury

30535 comes west through Bournemouth; MPD on left with 34021 DARTMOOR in the yard, 19 June 1961. Norman Preedy.

30536

To traffic as 535 26/10/38
Renumbered 30536 30/6/50

Works

16/10/41-3/12/41**A**	86,255	

Single lever controlling the reverser 280 monel metal stays riveted over & 280 nuts renewed 2 new fusible plugs 158 second hand small tubes welded

3/8/43-31/8/43**C**	47,405 Bricklayers Arms
9/9/44-19/1/45**A**	71,356 Brighton

Standard reverser re fitted 443 copper stays renewed 118 monel metal stays riveted over & 118 holes bushed 20 roof stays & 20 roof nuts renewed Throat plate grooving electric Barrel & Dome cleaned welding 158 new small tubes 'Howell' 21 superheater tubes repaired 21 new ferrules

4/3/47-11/4/47**C**	54,237 Bournemouth

Copper stays repaired in fire area 158 small tubes renewed

6/1947	Experimental tender cab fitted
9/1947	Tender cab removed
6/11/47-29/11/47**A**	63,471

Lemaitre blastpipe large diameter chimney

4/1948	Test No.1977: Water gauge protection fitted by Motive Power Depot
26/5/50-30/6/50**LI**	54,274

Renumbered 30536

21/8/52-20/9/52**GO**	105,621
23/4/54-15/5/54**LI-HI**	39,984

Tender sides and hand rails modified to E.46477

11/11/55-26/11/55**LC**	75,975
6/1/56-14/1/56**LC**	77,098
28/9/56-27/10/56**GO**	92,841

All monel metal stays and all roof stays renewed New copper firebox 2 new fusible plugs 158 new small tubes 'Stewart & Lloyds' 21 new superheater tubes

13/3/58-22/3/58**LC**	41,408

2 new fusible plugs 13 renewed second hand small tubes 21 new superheater tubes

23/3/59-18/4/59**LI-HI**	66,803

Pins fitted to regulator link in place of cir clips 310 monel metal stays repaired & 310 new nuts 2 new fusible plugs 158 new small tubes 'Stewart & Lloyds' 3 new superheater tubes

30/11/60-10/12/60**NC-LC**	99,853
13/6/61-29/7/61**GO**	107,387

AWS Blowdown gear & silencer Briquette tube feeder Spark arrester BR class 4 chimney & blastpipe Front buffer beam gusset strengthened 440 monel metal stays 1 transverse stay & 580 nuts renewed Copper tube 2 insert patches fitted & welded Firehole 2 new fusible plugs19 rivets renewed 158 new small tubes 'Stewart & Lloyds' 21 new superheater tubes

11/12/62-12/12/62**NC**	30,923

Snow plough attachments

Boilers

No.1070	from new
No.1067	29/11/47
No.1080	20/9/52
No.1068	27/10/56
No.1078	29/7/61

Tender

No.1919	from new

Sheds

Eastleigh	12/11/38
Redhill	by 1942
Eastleigh	15/6/46
Three Bridges	25/1/63

Withdrawn 5/1/64 Three Bridges shed.

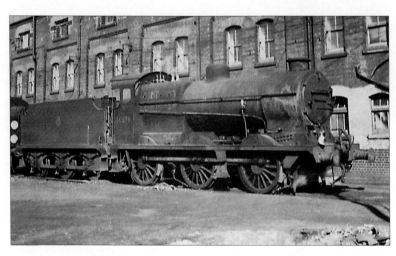

A very shabby 30536 at Eastleigh on 5 March 1961, looking very much in need of the General that began a few weeks later.

30536 with a short train of vans, at Weymouth in June 1962.

Three Bridges-bound 30536 running into Grange Road (between East Grinstead and Three Bridges) making for an idyllic little scene. The date is not known but it is certainly after the BR chimney was fitted in January 1961 and, given the location, almost certainly during its last working period, at Three Bridges, January 1963-January 1964. It still has the shed plate of its previous abode, 71A Eastleigh but as we see repeatedly, the SR did not bother overmuch with shed plates in these last years. To the left are the eaves surely, of the signalbox and adding to the exquisite portrait is the lad waiting inside the gate, the homely little crossing itself, the gorgeous lamp for walking across at night and the pub of course – *The Royal Oak* which, it seems, is still there. At least, we fervently hope so.

30537

To traffic as 537 26/10/38
Renumbered 30537 30/10/48

Works

30/12/38-6/1/39**D**	677	
18/8/42-19/9/42**A**	97,734	
7/1/43-20/1/43**C**	1,519	
13/10/43-28/10/43**C**	9,768 Redhill	
26/1/46-16/2/46**A**	74,329	

Test No.1964 Modified brick arch large chimney and jet blastpipe Set new small tubes 'Howell' Superheaters expanded & re-ferruled Test No.2014 Circlip on reversing handle collar Drg. W.6675 2 new fusible plugs

30/9/47-15/10/47**C**	42,433 Guildford	

Wasted stay nuts renewed copper stays re-riveted All small tubes renewed Superheater tubes expanded & re-ferruled

4/10/48-30/10/48**A**	59,700	

Renumbered 30537 612 monel metal stays renewed 2 fusible plugs & Brick arch studs renewed Set new small tubes 'Tubes Ltd' Set new superheater tubes

14/8/50-31/8/50**HC**	41,179	
7/9/51-29/9/51**LI**	60,915	

150 monel metal stays repaired Patch on top ½ of firehole Set new small tubes 'Howell' 3 new superheaters

4/7/52-11/7/52**LC**	79,312	

Copper tube 12 studs renewed 2 new fusible plugs

7/12/53-7/1/54**GO**	108,523	

Fire hole door modified Tender hand rails modified 10 monel metal stays renewed & 436 repaired 2 new fusible plugs Protection patch fitted to smokebox tube Set new small tubes 'Stewart & Lloyds' Set new superheater tubes

8/7/55-28/7/55**LC**	32,105 Brighton	

9 new small tubes 'Stewart & Lloyds'

21/1/57-16/3/57**GO**	58,646	

Modified fire doors & handrails 344 nuts renewed 2 new fusible plugs 158 new small tubes

2/7/59-8/8/59**LI-HI**	44,760	

Collar & split pins fitted to regulator link pins in place of cir clips 2 new fusible plugs 38 new small tubes 'Stewart and Lloyds' 3 new superheater tubes

28/11/60-29/12/60**LC**	Norwood Jct	

158 new small tubes

Boilers

No.1071	from new
No.1085	19/9/42
No.1084	16/2/46
No.1082	30/10/48
No.1064	16/3/57

Tender

No.1911	from new

Sheds

Bournemouth	12/11/38
Eastleigh	9/1939
Redhill	by 1942
Norwood Jct	31/7/48
Stewarts Lane	22/6/54
Norwood Jct	31/10/54
Brighton	4/1/62
Stewarts Lane	30/6/62

Withdrawn 8/12/62 Stewarts Lane shed.

30537 with small first emblem in May 1957 has even enjoyed a recent encounter with the Norwood Junction cleaning gang – an unusual event in the life of any Q.

30537, the only one not to get AWS, forging along with a freight at Eridge, 9 June 1962. D.C. Ovenden, ColourRail

30538

To traffic as 538 8/11/38
Renumbered 30538 24/12/48

Works

28/1/42-18/3/42**A**	96,546	
	200 monel metal stays riveted over 200 nuts renewed 2 new fusible plugs 158 second hand small tubes welded	
5/2/44-26/2/44**B**	43,926	
	21 copper & 92 steel stays renewed 2 new fusible plugs Superheater tubes expanded	
21/11/44-15/2/45**C**	63,188 Bricklayers Arms	
	Extension of mileage 5,000 158 new small tubes 21 new superheater tubes	
23/9/46-12/10/46**A**	97,296	
	Test No. 2032 Piston valves fitted to Drg W.7013 Lemaitre blastpipe large diameter chimney 622 monel metal stays renewed 90 holes bushed 158 new small tubes 'Howell' 21 new superheater tubes	
24/11/48-24/12/48**B**	50,709	
	Renumbered 30538 18 monel metal stays renewed 350 steel stays riveted over 350 nuts renewed ½ firehole patch 2 new fusible plugs Set second hand small tubes	
6/11/50-2/12/50**GO**	85,094	
	72 copper 31 monel metal & 160 roof stays renewed Top half of fire hole patch 158 new small tubes 'Howell' 21 new superheater tubes	
2/5/52-24/5/52**HI**	33,672	
	200 monel metal stays caulked 200 nuts renewed 2 new fusible plugs Foundation ring corner rivets renewed 158 new small tubes 'Howell' 21 new superheater tubes	
5/1/53-4/2/53**LC**	42,459	
	New cylinders	
20/4/53-25/4/53**LC**	46,262	
15/12/54-16/2/55**GO**	77,889 Brighton	
	4 no.62 piston rings All monel metal transverse & roof stays renewed New copper firebox Set new small tubes 'Tubes Ltd' 21 new superheater tubes	
7/11/56-1/12/56**LI-HI**	36,156	
	82 monel metal stays riveted over & 82 nuts renewed Copper tube seams caulked 2 new fusible plugs Foundation Ring 32 rivets repaired 158 small tubes second hand 3 new superheater tubes	
24/9/59-24/10/59**GO**	89,161	
	Regulator pins in place of cir clips Vacuum exhaust pipe drain to Drg. E.51347 All monel metal & roof stays renewed New copper firebox 130 holes bushed 2 new fusible plugs 158 new small tubes 'Stewart & Lloyds' 21 new superheater tubes	
11/10/61-28/10/61**LC**	34,625	
	Spark arrester AWS BR class 4 chimney and blastpipe	

Boilers

No.1072	from new
No.1074	12/10/46
No.1075	2/12/50
No.1070	16/2/55
No.1077	24/10/59

Tenders

No.1902	from new
No.1910	21/3/52 at Eastleigh shed
No.1916	11/12/52 at Three Bridges shed

Sheds

Bournemouth	10/12/38
Eastleigh	9/1939
Horsham	by 1942
Redhill	by 5/1945
Stewarts Lane	22/6/54
Norwood Jct	31/10/54
Brighton	18/3/61
Stewarts Lane	30/6/62
Bournemouth	30/12/62

Withdrawn 14/7/63 Bournemouth shed.

30538 finished life with a BR style chimney and finished up stored in the roundhouse at Fratton. Withdrawn from Bournemouth in July 1963 it was taken here – or took itself here – to languish for a couple of months before eventually departing for scrap – to Wards of Killamarsh it is said. RailOnline

Passenger work for 30538 waiting at Guildford to work east to Redhill on 1 April 1958. The electric unit 2693 is of interest, being one of the seven 'tin' 2-HAL units built in 1948 to Bulleid 4-SUB outline and not normally found on an up Portsmouth slow. They tended to congregate on the Victoria-Gatwick service; usually forming the rear unit on a down all-stations Brighton to be detached at Gatwick Airport, then re-attached at the front of the train on the up journey. They used to carry a side board stating GATWICK AIRPORT SERVICES. ColourRail

In familiar haunts; Norwood Junction in 1959. There were six Qs at the shed there that year. RailOnline

30539

To traffic as 539 6/12/38
Renumbered 30539 24/12/48

Works

3/10/42	Ashford
	25 copper & 243 monel metal stays riveted over 243 nuts renewed 2 new fusible plugs Copper tube 20 studs in flanges 158 new small tubes 'Talbot & Stead' 21 second hand superheater tubes
1/2/44-8/2/44**C**	28,864
	310 monel metal stays riveted over 310 nuts renewed Copper firehole seams caulked 2 new fusible plugs
8/6/44-1/7/44**C**	36,886
	27 copper stays renewed 210 monel metal stays riveted over 210 nuts renewed 2 new fusible plugs 158 new small tubes 'Howell'
28/1/46-23/2/46**A**	77,753
	40 monel metal stays renewed & 500 repaired & new nuts fitted 158 new small tubes 'Howell' Set new superheater tubes Test No.1967 Large chimney jet blast pipe and modified brick arch Ref T25/23/1967
30/10/46-16/11/46**C**	18,411
22/10/47-9/11/47**C**	43,454 Guildford
	Wasted stay nuts renewed 158 new small tubes 'New steel' Superheater tubes expanded beaded & re-ferruled
27/11/48-24/12/48**A**	63,450
	Renumbered 30539 520 monel metal stays renewed & 50 repaired 80 holes bushed Set new small tubes 'Talbot Stead' Set new superheater tubes
24/5/51-16/6/51**HI**	47,167
	280 monel metal stays repaired 280 nuts renewed 23 crown rivets renewed 2 new fusible plugs Firehole 19 new rivets Set new small tubes 3 new superheater tubes
14/1/53-7/2/53**GO**	83,575
	All monel metal stays riveted over All roof stays renewed New copper firebox Set new small tubes Set new superheater tubes
23/11/53-28/11/53**NC**	17,154
26/7/55-13/8/55**LI-HI**	50,030
	Tender handrails modified to to Drg. E.46477 420 monel metal stays riveted over 420 nuts renewed 2 new fusible plugs Copper firehole seams caulked casing covering 30 stay holes bushed Set new small tubes 'Stewart & Lloyds' Set new superheater tubes
24/12/57-25/1/58**GO**	109,910
	879 monel metal stays & 879 nuts renewed 20 crown stays renewed Copper firehole new back plate 100 second hand small tubes & 58 welded 21 new superheater tubes
4/5/60-21/5/60**LI-HI**	47,774
	AWS Blowdown gear & silencer Briquette tube feeder to tender 10 copper & 220 monel metal stays riveted over 220 nuts renewed Copper tube seams & 6 studs repaired Copper firehole seams & 40 studs repaired2 new fusible plugs 32 new small tubes 'Stewart & Lloyds' 3 new superheater tubes

Boilers

No.1073	from new
No.1085	23/2/46
No.1084	24/12/48
No.1072	7/2/53
No.1084	25/1/58

Tenders

No.1906	from new
No.1907	12/1/63 at Eastleigh shed

Sheds

Bournemouth	7/1/39
Eastleigh	9/1939
Horsham	by 1942
Eastleigh	by 5/1945
Redhill	15/6/46
Norwood Jct	31/7/48
Bournemouth	16/9/55

Withdrawn 13/1/63 Bournemouth shed.

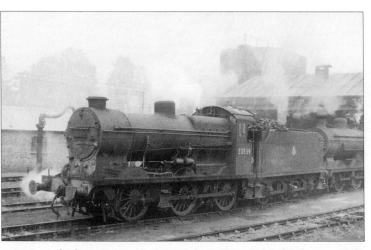

30539 on shed at Norwood, 24 October 1953. Behind it is one of the shed's 0-6-0 stalwarts, a Brighton C2X 'Vulcan'. At 2F, these were less powerful than the Qs. H.C. Casserley, courtesy M. Casserley.

30539 at London Bridge on 27 August 1949. After some time at Redhill it had moved to Norwood in July 1948; the 27th of August was a Saturday, so it likely that it finds itself here on some form of excursion work. When the snifting valves on the smokebox were first removed, the aperture was replaced by a circular blanking plate, visible here. H.C. Casserley, courtesy M. Casserley.

30539 at Poole station with a train for Bournemouth on 15 July 1960. Large second emblem now, with the rare right-facing lion. The view is from the station footbridge looking over Towngate Street towards High Street level crossing. The station is behind the photographer. This could well be a service from Swanage with previous tender-first running, given the tarpaulin or it might just be a hot day and the crew needed a bit of shade! H.C. Casserley, courtesy M. Casserley.

30540

To traffic as 540 31/12/38
Renumbered 30540 18/3/49

Works

11/3/41-29/3/41**C**	Guildford
	Extension of mileage 10,000 152 new small tubes
16/12/42-2/2/43**A**	96,534
	66 copper stays renewed 350 stays riveted over 350 nuts renewed 2 new fusible plugs 152 new small tubes 'Jarrow' 21 new superheater tubes
16/8/43-4/9/43**C**	6,225
6/10/43-1/12/43**B**	7,329
	Boiler off for fitters damaged frame
26/5/44	Ashford
24/1/47-18/4/47**B**	79,277 New Cross
19/12/47-17/1/48**A**	89,919
	Lemaitre blastpipe large diameter chimney 630 monel metal stays renewed 100 holes bushed 2 copper angle patches on Back Plate 158 new small tubes 'New Tubes Ltd'
22/2/49-18/3/49**LI**	30,198
	Renumbered 30540
22/12/49-20/1/50**LI**	48,894
	6 copper stays renewed 400 monel metals stays riveted over 400 nuts renewed All crown stays renewed Brick arch studs 2 fusible plugs renewed Set new small tubes 'Howell' Set new superheater tubes
25/6/51-6/7/51**LC**	85,471
	204 monel metal stays repaired 2 fusible plugs & brick arch studs renewed Set small tubes repaired
22/2/52-22/3/52**GO**	100,783
	All monel metal stays repaired 190 holes bushed New copper firebox Set new small tubes Set new superheater tubes
16/12/53-5/2/54**LI**	41,792 Brighton
	4 No.64 piston rings fitted Copper tubeplate 28 rivets replaced by stays 158 new small tubes supplied by Eastleigh Works
21/12/56-26/1/57**GO**	101,461
	51 copper & 421 monel metal stays renewed 575 nuts renewed Copper tube rivets replaced by studs 2 new fusible plugs Foundation ring 40 rivets repaired 158 new small tubes 'Stewart & Lloyds' 21 new superheater tubes
29/12/59-23/1/60**HI**	53,531
	BR type ATC fitted 260 monel metal stays & 260 nuts renewed 80 copper stays riveted over Copper tube 56 studs & seams repaired 2 fusible plugs renewed Firehole 18 rivets renewed 156 new small tubes 'Stewart & Lloyds' 3 new superheater tubes
29/11/60-17/12/60**HC**	66,201

Boilers

No.1074	from new
No.1077	2/2/43
No.1066	17/1/48
No.1064	22/3/52
No.1085	26/1/57

Tender

No.1908	from new

Sheds

Guildford	7/1/39
Horsham	by 1942
Three Bridges	1/4/48
Norwood Jct	20/7/53
Three Bridges	8/12/61

Withdrawn 24/11/62 Three Bridges shed.

540 at Guildford on 25 June 1939; viewed from the rear that Maunsell cab is seen to have been particularly generously-proportioned.

Back at Guildford twenty years later, on 3 May 1958; Bulleid chimney.

30541

To traffic as 541 February 1939
Renumbered 30541 9/48

Works

3/1941	Guildford shed
	150 new small tubes
17/10/42	235 monel metal stays caulked 235 nuts renewed 8 studs in flanges 2 new fusible plugs Set of second hand small tubes Set second hand superheater tubes
14/12/46	Lemaitre blastpipe large diameter chimney
14/4/52-14/6/52**GO**	198 holes bushed New copper firebox All monel metal & roof stays renewed 198 holes bushed Set new small tubes & new superheater tubes
11/1/54-21/1/54**LC**	37,048
17/11/54-4/12/54**LI**	56,503
	Tender doors & hand rails modified to Drg. E46477 144 steel stays riveted over 144 nuts renewed 2 new fusible plugs Set new small tubes 'Howell' 3 new superheater tubes
9/3/56-7/4/56**LC-HC**	87,058
5/8/57-17/8/57**GO**	120,255
	203 monel metal stays & 351 nuts renewed Seams chipped & caulked 2 new fusible plugs Set new small tubes 'Stewart & Lloyds' 21 new superheater tubes
6/7/59-8/8/59**LI-HI**	52,842
	Collar & regulator link pins fitted with split pins in place of cir clips 10 copper & 220 monel metal stays repaired 230 nuts renewed Copper tube 18 rivets replaced with studs 2 new fusible plugs 30 new small tubes 'Stewart & Lloyds' 3 new superheater tubes
26/2/62-24/3/62**LI**	107,379
	AWS Blowdown gear & silencer Briquette tube feeder Spark arrester gear 8 copper & 360 monel metal stays riveted over 360 nuts renewed 2 new fusible plugs Foundation ring 60 rivets repaired 30 new small tubes 'Stewart & Lloyds' 3 new superheater tubes
21/2/63-25/2/63**NC**	125,983
	Snow plough details fitted

NB. Spark arrester fitted at Bournemouth mpd Corr. ref. C51/1243 [no date available]

Boilers

No.1075	from new
No.1076	15/6/52

Tender

No.1909	from new

Sheds

Guildford	4/3/39
Horsham	by 1942
Three Bridges	27/12/47
Stewarts Lane	20/7/53
Bournemouth	1/10/53
Basingstoke	30/1/63
Guildford	1/4/63

30541 resplendent in new coat of black and second emblem at Eastleigh MPD after that 1957 General, on 25 August. Ken Fairey was in the same party as R.C. Riley – see page 13! Ken Fairey, ColourRail

Withdrawn 29/11/64 Guildford shed.
Preserved on Bluebell Railway.

54

30541 with traditional coating of BR grime, at Eastleigh on 6 July 1957. With cleared tender, it has been readied for entry to the works for a General overhaul. The Record puts the duration of this General at only twelve days – impossibly brief but sometimes dates were 'finessed' for internal accounting reasons. Nevertheless, the General *was* accomplished promptly, well within six weeks – see repainted 30541 next. Rail Online

30541 shunting mineral wagons at Lymington (the little shed and its water tank is alongside) on 18 July 1960. Withdrawn from Guildford, it was eventually tripped all the way to South Wales only to stand in Woodhams yard from February 1965 to 1973, when it was rescued for £3,250. It is now on the Bluebell Railway. H.C. Casserley, courtesy M. Casserley.

30542

To traffic as 542 22/2/39
Renumbered 30542 8/5/48

Works

10/4/41-2/5/41**C**	Guildford shed
	158 new small tubes
21/7/43	Damaged by enemy action Repaired to WO2135740 27 monel metal stays riveted over Copper firehole patches fitted on rhs of wrapper Firehole rivets hammered Barrel cleaned holes welded Set new small tubes 'Howell' Superheater tubes repaired steel with copper ends
11/6/46-29/6/46**C**	Horsham
14/4/48-8/5/48**A**	94,926
	Renumbered 30542 Lemaitre blastpipe large diameter chimney 70 copper stays renewed 250 monel metal stays repaired & all direct stays renewed 2 new fusible plugs Set new small tubes 'Tubes Ltd' Set new superheater tubes
6/5/49-10/5/49	24,355 Guildford
	Copper stays in Fire area re-riveted Stay nuts fitted to steel stays on tube plate Top of firehole caulked 31 second hand small tubes remainder expanded & beaded back Superheater tubes expanded & referruled
20/9/49-4/10/49**LC**	33,359
21/6/50-18/8/50**HI**	58,039
	470 monel metal stays caulked & nuts renewed Firehole welded & rivets renewed 2 new fusible plugs Set new small tubes & superheater tubes
18/4/52-26/4/52**LC**	92,326
	2 new monel metal stays & 60 repaired 2 copper firehole studs Small tubes & superheater tubes rerolled & rebeaded
14/1/53-7/2/53**GO**	109,877
	380 monel metal stays repaired & 380 nuts renewed 2 new fusible plugs Protection patch fitted Set new small tubes & superheater tubes Rivets in crown of back plate renewed with studs
24/9/54-2/10/54**LC**	39,185
15/2/55-12/4/55**HI**	46,362 Brighton
	5 copper stays renewed 36 monel metal stays riveted over 36 nuts renewed All roof stays & roof nuts renewed Copper firehole 18 collar bolts 2 new fusible plugs 158 new small tubes [supplied by Eastleigh] 21 new superheater tubes
26/6/57-13/7/57**LI-HI**	96,823
	358 monel metal stays repaired 358 nuts renewed 2 new fusible plugs Foundation ring 15 rivets renewed 158 new small tubes 'Stewart & Lloyds' 21 new superheater tubes
30/12/58-24/1/59**GO**	139,391
	Split pin & collar fitted to regulator pin in place of cir clips 326 monel metal stays & 528 nuts Copper patch welded on Firehole lap renewed 158 new small tubes 'Stewart & Lloyds'
17/6/61-9/9/61**LC**	Norwood Jct
	158 new small tubes & 21 new superheater tubes
7/2/62-3/3/62**LI**	60,710
	AWS Blowdown gear & silencer Briquette tube feeder Vacuum exhaust pipe & elbow 1 monel metal stay renewed 10 copper & 290 monel metal stays riveted over 290 nuts renewed 2 new plugs Foundation ring 32 rivets repaired 30 new small tubes 'Stewart & Lloyds' 3 new superheater tubes 21 ferrules renewed
28/11/62-30/11/62**NC**	74,724
	Copper tube seams & 48 studs recaulked Attachment for snow plough BR type ATC E51347 vacuum exhaust drain pipes

Boilers

No.1076	from new
No.1083	8/5/48
No.1077	7/2/53
No.1074	24/1/59

Tenders

No.1910	from new
No.1902	21/3/52 at Eastleigh shed

Sheds

Guildford	22/2/39
Horsham	by 1942
Three Bridges	27/12/47
Horsham	1/4/48
Tunbridge W W	31/5/48
Eastleigh	9/9/50
Guildford	17/12/62

Withdrawn 20/12/64 Guildford shed.

30542 out on its own on one of the long sidings leading to the turntable at Bournemouth shed, 17 July 1958. A.E. West, courtesy Mike King.

30542 at Guildford shed, 28 September 1964; AWS fitted. On this one Q, the two bolted plates at the front under the smokebox door which could be removed to afford access to the cylinder heads and piston rods are missing the distinctive handles. There's always one! Small modifications to front framing indicate it has been modified to take a snow plough. ColourRail

30543

To traffic as 543 28/3/39
Renumbered 30543 3/4/48

Works

31/5/41	Guildford
	Extension of mileage 5,000 152 new small tubes
25/9/42-21/10/42**A**	97,701
	250 steel stays riveted over 250 nuts renewed 2 new fusible plugs
27/2/48-3/4/48**A**	97,108
	Renumbered 30543 Lemaitre blastpipe large diameter chimney 610 new monel metal stays 140 holes bushed 2 new fusible plugs Set new small tubes 'Howell' Set new superheater tubes
21/10/49-15/11/49**LC**	38,431 Guildford
14/3/50-14/4/50**LC**	40,931
	50 monel metal stays repaired & 50 nuts renewed Internal tube & firehole plates-seams repaired Small tubes repaired Set new Superheater tubes
5/1/51-3/2/51**A**	60,407
	823 monel metal stays renewed Copper wrapping new ½ sides 158 new small tubes 'Howell' Barrel new 21 new superheater tubes
24/2/53-14/3/53**GO**	55,861
	10 new monel metal stays & 240 repaired 240 new nuts Copper wrapper ½ sides welded 2 new fusible plugs Set new small tubes & new superheater tubes
18/2/55-12/3/55**GO**	46,085
	Modified cab doors & hand rails to Drg E.46477 22 copper & 460 monel metal stays renewed All roof stays repaired New copper firehole Set new small tubes 'Stewart & Lloyds' Set new superheater tubes
10/12/55	68 copper stays repaired 20 copper riveted over116 nuts renewed Copper Tube 24 studs repaired 3 superheater tubes ferrules repaired [**Engine not booked into shops for this repair**]
29/5/57-22/6/57**LI-HI**	58,245
	95 copper & 302 monel metal stays riveted over 306 nuts renewed 2 new fusible plugs 158 new small tubes 'Stewart & Lloyds' 21 new superheater tubes
28/10/57-9/11/57**LC-HC**	65,186
	65 copper & 39 monel metal stays riveted over Foundation ring 14 rivets repaired Boiler lifted from frame for repair of stays behind frame then replaced
3/11/59-28/11/59**GO**	103,815
	BR type ATC 922 copper stays & 922 nuts renewed 20 roof stays renewed 276 holes bushed [Bottom of steel tube plate to renew] 2 new fusible plugs 158 new small tubes 'Stewart & Lloyds' 21 new superheater tubes
12/10/61-4/11/61**LC**	39,844
	Spark arrester gear BR class 4 chimney and blastpipe 2 new fusible plugs 158 new small tubes 'Stewart & Lloyds' 3 new superheater tubes
18/12/61-22/12/61**LC**	39,844
13/3/62-7/4/62**HI**	44,986
	Blowdown gear & silencer Briquette tube feeder 8 copper & 350 monel metal stays riveted over 350 nuts renewed 2 fusible plugs renewed 30 new small tubes 'Stewart & Lloyds' 3 new superheater tubes
23/11/62-24/11/62**NC**	55,072
	Snow plough fitted

Boilers

No.1077	from new
No.1082	21/10/42
No.1068	3/4/48
No.1071	3/2/51
No.1084	14/3/53
No.1065	12/3/55
No.1083	28/11/59

Tender

No.1915	from new

Sheds

Guildford	29/4/39
Horsham	by 1942
Tunbridge W W	31/5/48
Eastleigh	9/9/50
Stewarts Lane	17/12/62
Three Bridges	30/12/62
Brighton	6/1/64
Redhill	25/5/64

Withdrawn 20/12/64 Redhill shed.

30543 at Eastleigh, 15 May 1954. Norman Preedy.

30543 on the turntable at Guildford shed in the period between getting a BR chimney (November 1961) and withdrawal at the end of 1964. Second BR emblem. RailOnline

30544

To traffic as 544 25/4/39
Renumbered S544 6/3/48; 30544 25/3/50

Works

3/1941	Guildford
	148 new small tubes & 15 second hand
2/4/43	203 nuts renewed 2 new fusible plugs Flanges caulked Barrel cleaned Set new small tubes 'Howell' Superheater tubes new steel with copper ends
16/7/46	Lemaitre blastpipe large diameter chimney
28/2/48-6/3/48	Renumbered S544 616 new monel metal stays 110 holes bushed Top half copper firehole welded 2 new fusible plugs & brick arch studs renewed 152 new small tubes 'Howell' 21 second hand superheater tubes
17/6/49	150 monel metal stays repaired Firebox studs & seams caulked 2 new fusible plugs Small tubes expanded Superheater tubes expanded & re-ferruled
25/3/50	Renumbered 30544 370 monel metal & 24 roof stays renewed 50 holes bushed 2 fusible plugs Brick arch studs renewed
12/1/53-6/3/53**LI**	Brighton
	14 monel metal stays renewed 88 copper & 110 monel metal stays riveted over 110 nuts renewed 7 roof stays & 7 roof nuts renewed 2 new fusible plugs 2 angle patches on back plate158 new tubes supplied by Eastleigh Works 21 new superheater tubes
20/4/54-14/5/54**NC-LC**	90,882 Brighton
7/9/55-1/10/55**GO**	119,384
	Modified fire door fitted Tender hand rails modified to Drg.46477 All monel metal & roof stays renewed New copper firebox 2 new fusible plugs Set new small tubes 'Stewart & Lloyds' Set new superheater tubes
21/11/57-21/12/57**LI**	58,145 Ashford
	325 nuts renewed Copper tube 24 studs fitted & flanges caulked 2 new fusible plugs 158 new small tubes 3 superheater tubes repaired & 18 expanded & re-ferruled
16/9/58-25/10/58**LC**	78,116
4/8/60-3/9/60**GO**	121,607
	AWS gear Vacuum exhaust pipe drain Split pins & collar to regulator link pins in place of cir clips All steel & all roof stays renewed 200 holes bushed New copper firebox 2 new fusible plugs Casing covering 2 casing sides to fit & weld 158 new small tubes 'Stewart & Lloyds' 21 new superheater tubes
28/8/62-15/9/62**LC**	37,146
	Spark arrester gear

Boilers

No.1078	from new
No.1077	6/3/48
No.1081	25/3/50
No.1078	1/10/55
No.1065	3/9/60

Tender

No.1912	from new

Sheds

Guildford	27/5/39
Horsham	by 1942
Tunbridge W W	31/5/48
Eastleigh	9/9/50
Three Bridges	19/3/52
Stewarts Lane	20/7/53
Horsham	1/10/53
Three Bridges	18/7/59
Brighton	26/5/61
Stewarts Lane	30/6/62
Three Bridges	30/1/62

Withdrawn 5/1/64 Three Bridges shed.

London Bridge, 8 May 1962. 30544 is in Platform 8, one of the three low level terminal platforms of the SECR station (the high level is 1-6 on the right, although one of the platforms disappeared early on). The headcode is London Bridge-New Cross Gate via Bricklayers Arms Junction, so is probably a van train or empty stock. A healthy selection of vans – LNER fitted goods van, BR full brake, LMS full brake, LNER full brake, possibly a Southern utility van and then maybe coaches until it becomes a bit fuzzy. L. Rowe, ColourRail

30544 at Fratton on 16 March 1958. The small emblem indicates a tender change since 1955, not noted in the Record. Norman Preedy.

30545

To traffic as 545 3/6/39
Renumbered 30545 4/49

Works

5/1941		Guildford
		143 new small tubes 21 second hand superheater tubes
3/2/43		228 steel stays riveted over 228 nuts renewed 2 fusible plugs 158 second hand small tubes 21 second hand superheater tubes
7/6/46		608 copper stays renewed 60 stay holes welded Set new tubes 'Howell' Set new superheater tubes
22/4/49		renumbered 30545 360 monel metal stays repaired over 360 nuts renewed Firebox seams caulked & studs repaired Top ½ firehole welded 2 fusible plugs 158 new small tubes 'Howell' 21 new superheater tubes
8/2152		All monel metal & all roof stays renewed 643 holes bushed New copper firebox Set new small tubes & superheater tubes
14/1/54-5/3/54**LI**		49,334 Brighton
		2 fusible plugs 158 new small tubes & 6 new superheater tubes
29/3/56-28/4/56**LI-HI**		97,694
		244 monel metal stays repaired 244 nuts renewed 30 rivets in flanges replaced by studs 2 fusible plugs Firehole 45 corner rivets replaced 158 new small tubes 'Stewart & Lloyds' 12 new superheater tubes
11/3/58-18/4/58**GO**		149,467
		Blowdown valve & operating gear BR class 4 chimney & blastpipe Briquette container fitted to tender Vacuum exhaust pipe drain Split pins & collars to regulator link pins in place of circlips 293 monel metal stays 401 nuts & 160 crown stays renewed 2 fusible plugs Firehole 18 rivets renewed Foundation ring 65 rivets renewed 158 new small tubes 'Stewart & Lloyds' 21 new superheater tubes
26/8/58-5/9/58**NCreturn**		8,740
		Firehole welded and 17 rivets replaced
20/11/58-6/12/58**NCreturn**	14,847	
		29 monel metal stays & 29 nuts renewed Firehole 26 rivets renewed
22/3/60-2/4/60**LC**		48,789
		BR type ATC 91 monel metal stays riveted over 2 fusible plugs Firehole patch & 14 rivets repaired 6 second hand small tubes
13/12/60-14/1/61**LI-HI**		66,022
		335 steel stays riveted over 340 nuts renewed 2 fusible plugs Foundation ring 32 rivets repaired 32 new small tubes 'Tube Products' 3 new superheater tubes
23/2/62-3/3/62**NC-LC**		87,632
		Spark arrester gear
16/5/63-8/6/63**LC**		110,807
24/12/63-4/1/64**NC**		117,293
		Snowplough details marked off

Boilers

No.1079	from new
No.1074	3/2/43
No.1064	7/6/46
No.1074	8/2/52
No.1066	19/4/58

Tender

No.1914	from new

Sheds

Nine Elms	from new
Guildford	by 12/1942
Redhill	by 5/1945
Horsham	31/5/48
Three Bridges	18/7/59
Nine Elms	27/1/64

Withdrawn 18/4/65 Nine Elms shed.

Horsham's 30545 in the shed yard at Brighton; high train shed of the station at right, distinctive louvred roof of the works at the left. The date is not recorded but the BR chimney appeared in April 1958. The loco is working from Horsham which since 1959 had been sub to Three Bridges and in theory coded 75E – no one really bothered by this time and 30545 still carries the defunct shed plate of Horsham, 75D. AWS and its conduit prominent. Norman Preedy.

A good view to appreciate the vagaries of the lubricating oil feed pipes to the cylinders, steamchest and axleboxes; compare their winding paths with say, 30548 (with a Bulleid chimney, incidentally) in a very similar pose (again by Peter Groom) at Eastleigh on 26 August 1963, page 14. You could model them any way you like, really! Peter Groom.

30546

To traffic as 546 23/6/39
Renumbered 30546 8/49

Works

14/9/46	Lemaitre blastpipe large diameter chimney 610 monel metal & all roof stays renewed 200 holes bushed New fusible plugs & brick arch studs 158 new small tubes 'Howell' 21 new superheater tubes
16/7/47	Guildford
	Tube work only 158 new small tubes & superheater tubes expanded & referruled
27/1/50	208 monel metal stays repaired Firebox-top half of firehole welded 2 new fusible plugs
31/1/51	342 monel metal stays repaired Tube & firehole seams & studs caulked 2 new fusible plugs 158 new small tubes 'Howell' 21 new superheater tubes
7/5/53-30/5/53**GO**	360 monel metal stays riveted over 360 nuts renewed 2 new fusible plugs 158 new small tubes 'Howell' 21 new superheater tubes
30/8/55-8/11/55**HI**	54,885 Brighton
	4 no.64 piston rings 93 steel stays riveted over 93 steel stays & 93 nuts renewed 2 new fusible plugs Copper tube 9 collar bolts158 new small tubes 'Stewart & Lloyds' 3 new superheater tubes
10/5/57-25/5/57**LC**	92,509
	62 copper stays renewed 2 new fusible plugs 158 new small tubes 'Stewart & Lloyds'
8/11/57-7/12/57**GO**	103,895
	Briquette tube feeder to tender Blowdown valve & operating gear to engine
23/12/58-17/1/59**LC**	22,800
	Regulator valve rod pins Collar & split pins in place of cir clips
5/8/60-20/8/60**LI-HI**	55,593
	AWS Vacuum exhaust pipe drain at smokebox
28/6/61-6/7/61**NC-LC**	73,763
21/9/62-27/10/62**GO**	96,377
	425 monel metal stays & 425 nuts renewed 2 new fusible plugs Copper firehole right hand flanges & firehole lap renewed 158 new small tubes 'Stewart & Lloyds' 21 new superheater tubes

Boilers

No.1080	from new
No.1079	14/9/46
No.1069	27/1/50
No.1071	30/5/53
No.1067	7/12/57
No.1081	27/10/62

Tender

No.1916	from new
No.1910	2/53

Sheds

Nine Elms	22/7/39
Guildford	27/2/40
Reading	4/10/47
Redhill	27/12/47
Horsham	31/5/48
Three Bridges	18/7/59
Bournemouth	6/1/64

30546 with Bulleid chimney, at Eastbourne on 7 October 1950.
H.C. Casserley, courtesy M. Casserley.

Withdrawn 10/5/64 Bournemouth shed.

30546 stands at Eastleigh accompanied by a pile of oil drums on 25 June 1961. It is awaiting entry for an NC (Non Classified – usually out of course remedial attention) which, when further attention was found to be needed, was upgraded to LC Light Casual. 30546 subsequently underwent a late General, completed in 1962 only to be withdrawn some 18 months later. RailOnline

Happily 'mixed traffic' to the last, 30546 on 5 August 1963 with a train from Horsham approaching Itchingfield Junction going south from Christs' Hospital, heading for Brighton via the Steyning line – which is why the splitting distant signal is off. RailOnline

30547

To traffic as 547 22/7/39
Renumbered 30547 3/48

Works

11/3/42	Only date entered on Boiler Record card
4/1944	Eastleigh
	20 monel metal stays renewed 135 second hand small tubes
5/1/46	Lemaitre blastpipe large diameter chimney 450 monel metal stays riveted over 450 nuts renewed 2 new fusible plugs
15/10/47	New Cross Gate
	Studs renewed in right angle patch on tube plate 4 studs renewed in r & l angle patch on back plate 40 missing & wasted stay nuts renewed both sides in firebox & tube plate Set small tubes renewed 'New Steel' Superheater tubes expanded
13/3/48	Renumbered 30547 604 new monel metal stays 1 new tube plate stay Top half of firehole welded Drop plugs renewed 2 new fusible plugs 158 new small tubes 'Talbot Stead' 21 new superheater tubes
9/9/49	474 new monel metal stays 158 repaired & new nuts Top ½ of firehole welded & 16 fire hole rivets renewed
27/10/50	Ashford
	Set new small tubes 'Howell'
1/2/52	248 monel metal new stays & 229 repaired 577 nuts Copper tube rivets renewed with studs 2 new fusible plugs Set new small tubes
15/12/53-9/1/54**LI-HI**	39,561
	Tender hand rails modified 300 new monel metal stays & 300 new nuts 2 new fusible plugs Set of new small tubes & new superheater tubes
24/4/56-19/5/56**GO**	85,182
	All monel metal and roof stays renewed All nuts renewed 171 holes bushed New copper firebox 158 new small tubes 'Stewart & Lloyds' 21 new superheater tubes
23/4/58-17/5/58**LI-HI**	54,695
	Blowdown valve & operating gear Front buffer beam strengthened Briquette container fitted to tender 260 monel metal stays riveted over 260 nuts renewed 2 new fusible plugs Foundation Ring 38 rivets repaired 158 new small tubes 'Stewart & Lloyds' 3 new superheater tubes
15/11/60-26/11/60**LC**	102,280
17/3/61-1/4/61**NC-LC**	106,018
	AWS
27/9/61-28/10/61**GO**	113,425
	Spark arrester Front buffer beam gusset strengthened BR class 4 chimney & blastpipe 461 monel metal stays & 502 nuts renewed Copper tube 56 studs renewed 2 new fusible plugs 158 new small tubes 'Tube Products' 21 new Superheater tubes
13/12/62-29/12/62**LC**	24,771

Boilers

No.1081	from new
No.1068	5/1/46
No.1069	13/3/48
No.1073	9/9/49
No.1068	1/2/52
No.1081	19/5/56
No.1068	28/10/61

Tender

No.1913	from new

Sheds

Nine Elms	19/8/39
Eastleigh	27/2/40
Redhill	15/6/46
Three Bridges	31/5/48
Norwood Jct	12/5/51
Horsham	30/9/55
Three Bridges	18/7/59

Withdrawn 5/1/64 Three Bridges shed.

30547 occupying itself around Eastleigh. From the piles of clinker this looks like a spot where locos could pause for a while, the fireman taking the chance to sort the fire out a bit and bring coal forward.

30547 at Horsham shed; large second emblem, 4F and triangle on cabside. There is no date but the period is post-October 1961 when the BR chimney was put on. As mentioned before, the odd absence of a 'bash plate' seems to be peculiar to the Qs. The Qs (possibly not all of them) acquired foot plates on top of the buffer shanks late on. transporttreasury

30548

To traffic as 548 29/8/39
Renumbered 30548 22/12/50

Works

30/3/42-10/6/42**A**	75,323
17/6/43-24/6/43**D**	28,255
14/3/45-14/4/45**A**	79,600

74 copper stays renewed Rivets & seams caulked 2 new fusible plugs 158 second hand small tubes 21 second hand superheater tubes

10/10/47-2/11/47**A**	70,393

Lemaitre blastpipe large diameter chimney 592 monel metal stays renewed 80 holes bushed 2 new fusible plugs Brick arch studs renewed

23/11/50-22/12/50**HI**	84,782

Renumbered 30548 14 monel metal & 400 copper stays repaired 2 new fusible plugs Set of new small tubes 'Howell' Set of new Superheater tubes

6/10/52-1/11/52**LI**	131,648

360 steel stays repaired 2 new fusible plugs 30 new small tubes

4/12/53-24/12/53**GO**	165,929

2 new cylinders 388 monel metal stays & 640 nuts renewed All roof stays renewed New copper back plate 2 new fusible plugs Set new small tubes 'Talbot Stead' 21 new superheater tubes

15/5/56-2/6/56**LI**	61,568

162 monel metals stays riveted over 162 nuts renewed 2 new fusible plugs 30 second hand small tubes 3 new superheater tubes

2/9/58-27/9/58**GO**	114,905

All monel metal & roof stays renewed 160 holes bushed 2 new fusible plugs New copper firebox 158 new small tubes 'Universal' 21 new superheater tubes

10/3/61-1/4/61**LI**	52,669

AWS Blowdown gear silencer Briquette tube feeder to tender 10 copper & 275 monel metal stays riveted over 280 nuts renewed2 new fusible plugs 34 new small tubes 'Tube Products' 3 new superheater tubes

28/12/62-29/12/62**NC**	88,832

Snow plough attachments

Boilers

No.1082	from new
No.1084	10/6/42
No.1066	14/4/45
No.1065	2/11/47
No.1069	24/12/53
No.1071	27/9/58

Tender

No.1917	from new

Sheds

Nine Elms	16/9/39
Eastleigh	27/2/40
Bournemouth	3/1944
Three Bridges	30/12/62
Eastleigh	25/1/63

Withdrawn 21/3/65 Eastleigh Shed.

30548 crosses Canute Road with a freight out of Southampton Old Docks on 4 July 1959. transporttreasury

30548 with LSWR pull-push set 1 and van on the rear, at Brockenhurst on 20 May 1957. The train is about to leave for Bournemouth West via Ringwood (the old road) and must be a substitute for an M7 failure. H.C. Casserley, courtesy M. Casserley.

30548 in a pretty portrait at Poole, 20 May 1961. K. Fairey, ColourRail

30549

To traffic as 549 20/9/39
Renumbered 30549 8/4/49

Works

22/12/39-9/1/40**C**	4,461
20/3/41-9/4/41**C**	34,060
18/1/43-29/3/43**A**	89,461
	178 copper stays renewed 400 monel metal riveted over 400 nuts renewed 2 new fusible plugs 158 second hand small tubes 21 second hand superheater tubes
29/1/45-22/2/45**C**	56,793 Bournemouth
	Extension of mileage 5,000 137 new small tubes
16/4/46-11/5/46**A**	90,499
	Snifting valves removed and header blanked off 123 copper & 19 monel metal stays renewed New set of crown stays Top ½ of firehole welded 158 new small tubes 'Howell' Set new superheater tubes
1/3/49-8/4/49**A**	63,350
	Renumbered 30549 Lemaitre blastpipe large diameter chimney 8 copper & 628 monel metal stays renewed 50 holes bushed Top ½ firehole welded 158 new small tubes 'Talbot Stead' 21 new superheater tubes
20/2/50-3/3/50**LC**	22,205
30/12/52-25/2/53**LI**	94,567 Brighton
	132 monel metal stays caulked 132 nuts renewed Copper tube plate 16 collar bolts Copper firehole 32 collar bolts 2 new fusible plugs Firehole 15 new rivets 158 new small tubes 6 new superheater tubes
29/6/55-6/8/55**GO**	154,059
	Modified chimney & BR class 4 blastpipe Tender hand rails and fire door modified to Drg E.46477 721 monel metal stays renewed 308 holes bushed Copper tube copper firehole & copper wrapping all new 158 new small tubes 'Stewart & Lloyds' 21 new superheater tubes
29/7/57-10/8/57**LI-HI**	36,807
	300 monel metal stays & 315 nuts renewed Copper tube 68 studs repaired 2 new fusible plugs Foundation ring 30 rivets repaired158 new small tubes 'Stewart & Lloyds' 21 new superheater tubes
16/6/59-4/7/59**LC**	67,401 Ashford
19/10/60-19/11/60**GO**	88,179
	AWS Vacuum exhaust pipe at smokebox end Split pins to regulator valve links in place of cir clips 240 monel metal stays & 250 nuts renewed 2 new fusible plugs 158 new small tubes 'Stewart & Lloyds' 21 new superheater tubes

Boilers

No.1083	from new
No.1079	29/3/43
No.1073	11/5/46
No.1085	8/4/49
No.1075	6/8/55
No.1070	19/11/60

Tender

No.1894	from new

Sheds

Nine Elms	14/10/39
Eastleigh	27/2/40
Bournemouth	3/1944
Norwood Jct	16/9/55
Brighton	4/1/62
Stewarts Lane	30/6/62
Three Bridges	17/12/62

Withdrawn 21/7/63 Three Bridges shed.

The final Q, 30549 at Brighton MPD on 28 February 1953, in 'pre-spout' days. It has just undergone a Light Intermediate at the adjacent works. A Light Intermediate might not necessarily be expected to involve a full repaint but clearly that's what has happened here. transporttreasury

In the General of 29/6/55-6/8/55 30549 was transmogrified by this singularly unlovely 'spout', barely dignified by the official expression 'Modified chimney and BR class 4 blastpipe'. In fact it was merely the inner sleeving. Nothing if not cheap! Here it is on Eastleigh MPD immediately after the work, about to be emerge to a wider, shocked, world. Norman Preedy.

30549, now with large second emblem, at Norwood Junction MPD on 15 January 1961, in a line of locos readied to go off shed for their next jobs. The view is the traditional one from the little footbridge over the southbound 'Crystal Palace flyover'. It has been said that by the latter part of the 1930s when the Q 0-6-0s were built, the future was electric and steam locomotives were only to be built in the event of special need, where older types were too decrepit, or where future electrification was not imminent. They would only keep services going before the third rail could spread everywhere. Nevertheless Maunsell managed to build any number of 2-6-0s, 4-6-0s and 4-4-0s; then came Bulleid, who had quite obviously never heard of any of this, embarking as he did on the country's second-largest fleet of Pacifics. And of course there was the curious case of his singular 0-6-0s, the Q1s. Watch this space... RailOnline

The Knackers Yard
Disposal of Southern Workhorses 30530-30549
Courtesy the What Really Happened to Steam Group
(IW = In Week Ending)

30530 Withdrawn from Nine Elms 20.12.64.
Sold to T.W.Ward Grays. Despatched 12.4.65.
Stored Nine Elms 19.1.65-31.3.65.
Observed at breaker's yard 24.4.65.

30531 Withdrawn from Redhill 19.7.64.
Sold to P.Wood Queenborough*. Despatched 14.11.64.
Stored Redhill 2.8.64-14.11.64.

30532 Withdrawn from Salisbury 5.1.64. Sold from
Woodford Halse.
Sold to T.W.Ward – Killamarsh 24.10.64.
Stored Salisbury 7.4.64-9.8.64.
Stored Banbury 29.8.64-3.10.64.
Observed Woodford Halse 11.10.64.
Despatched from Woodford Halse 24.10.64.
Observed at breakers yard 15.11.64.

30533 Bournemouth loco, withdrawn Eastleigh
Works IW 30.3.63.
Cut up at Eastleigh Works IW 18.5.63.
Stored Eastleigh 10.3.63-21.4.63.
Observed at Eastleigh Works 12.5.63.

30534 Withdrawn from Stewarts Lane 22.12.62.
Sold to P.Wood Queenborough*.
Stored Stewarts Lane 13.1.63-8.12.63.

30535 Withdrawn from Guildford 25.4.65.
Sold to Bird's Commercial Motors Bridgend.
Despatched 6.9.65.
Stored Guildford 15.5.6-7.6.65.
Moved to Eastleigh 11.7.65.
Stored Eastleigh 11.7.65-15.8.65.
Observed at Eastleigh Works 28.8.65.
Despatched to Westbury 6.9.65.
Stored Westbury 6.9.65-2.10.65.
Observed Barrow Road 12.10.65.
Observed at breaker's yard 24.10.65-4.1.66.

30536 Withdrawn from Three Bridges 5.1.64.
Sold to T.W.Ward Killamarsh. Despatched 11.6.64.
Observed Three Bridges 30.1.64.
Observed at breaker's yard 21.6.64-24.10.64.

30537 Stewarts Lane loco withdrawn Eastleigh
Works IW 8.12.62.
Sold to P.Wood Queenborough*.
Stored Stewarts Lane 13.1.63-8.12.63.

30538 Bournemouth loco withdrawn Eastleigh Works 14.7.63.
Sold to T.W.Ward Killamarsh 24.10.64. Sold from
Woodford Halse.
Stored Fratton 7.9.63-5.8.64.
Stored Banbury 16.8.64-3.10.64.
Observed Woodford Halse 11.10.64.
Despatched from Woodford Halse 24.10.64.

30539 Bournemouth loco withdrawn Eastleigh Works 13.1.63.
Cut up at Eastleigh Works IW 22.6.63.
Stored Eastleigh 27.1.63-1.6.63.
Stored at Eastleigh Works 8.6.63-16.6.63.

30540 Withdrawn from Three Bridges IW 24.11.62.
Sold to P.Wood Queenborough*.
Stored Stewarts Lane 22.9.63-8.12.63.

30541 Withdrawn from Guildford 29.11.64. Sold from
Eastleigh.
Sold to Woodham Bros Barry. Despatched 23.2.65.
Stored Guildford 22.11.64-28.11.64.
Stored Eastleigh 8.1.65-14.2.65.
Observed Westbury 23.2.65.
Arrived at Barry 2.65.

30542 Withdrawn from Guildford 20.12.64. Sold from
Eastleigh.
Sold to Bird's Commercial Motors Morriston.
Despatched 28.4.65.
Stored Eastleigh 8.1.65-28.4.65.
Despatched to Barrow Road 28.4.65.
Observed Barrow Road 29.4.65.
Observed Swansea East Dock 5.5.65.

30543 Withdrawn from Redhill 20.12.64.
Sold from Nine Elms.
Sold to T.W.Ward Grays. Despatched 12.4.65.
Observed Nine Elms 31.3.65.

30544 Withdrawn from Three Bridges 5.1.64.
Sold to T.W.Ward Killamarsh. Despatched 11.6.64.
Observed at breaker's yard 21.6.64-27.9.64.

30545 Withdrawn from Nine Elms 18.4.65.
Sold to Bird's Commercial Motors Bynea.
Despatched 29.7.65.
Stored Nine Elms 17.4.65-6.6.65.
Observed Salisbury 29.7.65.
Observed Barrow Road 31.7.65.
Observed at breaker's yard 2.8.65-9.8.65.

30546 Withdrawn from Bournemouth 10.5.64.
Sold to R.A.King Norwich 10.7.64.
Stored Eastleigh 18.5.64-4.10.64.
Observed at Eastleigh Works 17.10.64.
Observed Cambridge 13.11.64.
Observed at breaker's yard 13.12.64-14.2.65.

30547 Withdrawn from Three Bridges 5.1.64.
Sold to T.W.Ward Killamarsh. Despatched 11.6.64.
Observed Three Bridges 30.1.64.
Observed at breaker's yard 27.6.64-22.8.64.

30548 Withdrawn from Eastleigh 21.3.65.
Sold to Cox & Danks Park Royal. Despatched 16.6.65.
Stored Eastleigh 6.3.65-13.6.65.
Observed at Eastleigh Works 16.6.65.

30549 Withdrawn from Three Bridges 21.7.63.
Sold to G.Cohen Kettering.
Stored Three Bridges 21.8.63-30.1.64.
Despatched to Clapham Junction yard 25.3.64.
Despatched to Cricklewood 26.3.64.
Stored Cricklewood 26.3.64-3.4.64.
Observed at breaker's yard 12.4.64 – 14.6.64.

*Reported as P Wood; actually 'Lacmots' Queenborough.